MEDIEVAL ENGLAND

Archaeological Collections in the Ashmolean Museum from Alfred the Great to Richard III

by

MOIRA HOOK
and
ARTHUR MACGREGOR

ASHMOLEAN MUSEUM, OXFORD
1997

CONTENTS

ACKNOWLEDGEMENTS

We are grateful to our colleague John Steane, who read the text in draft and made many valuable comments; he is also the source of the photograph forming Fig. 23. Fig. 77 is reproduced by courtesy of the Bodleian Library. Other photographs were produced by the Photographic Department of the Ashmolean, many taken especially for this publication by Nick Pollard, Jane Inskipp and Anne Holly. For drawings reproduced here we are pleased to thank Keith Bennett (Fig. 19), Nick Griffiths (Figs. 2, 80), Harry Lange (Figs. 20, 24) and Julian Munby (Fig. 38).

AN EMERGING STATE

Between the accession of Alfred to the throne of Wessex in 871 and the arrival of William of Normandy's all-conquering army in 1066, England evolved from a loose confederacy of kingdoms – Northumbria, Mercia, East Anglia and Wessex – to a single unified nation.

At the end of the eighth century, with the death of Offa, political power had shifted southwards from the kingdom of Mercia to the House of Wessex. Throughout this period Anglo-Saxon England was beset by land-hungry and gold-hungry Scandinavians. After ravaging East Anglia and all of eastern England, they invaded Northumbria and overran Mercia. Wessex too suffered at Danish hands, but determined campaigning by Alfred eventually brought success. In 878 Alfred routed the enemy at Edington, Wiltshire. Guthrum the Danish leader, in accepting peace terms, adopted the Christian faith, with Alfred standing as his godfather, and in eastern England a virtual Danish state was established – the Danelaw. There were more attacks in 892 and 896 but Alfred held firm and maintained his rule over Wessex, West Mercia and London, which he had occupied since 886.

But it was as a peacetime ruler that Alfred earned the title 'The Great'. He created fortified towns, established schools, imported scholars and craftsmen, encouraged the clergy and ordered the compilation of the *Anglo-Saxon Chronicle*, one of the primary sources for the history of England, which was to be continued for two centuries after his death.

Under Alfred's successor, Edward the Elder, English rule was established as far north as the Forth and Edgar, Alfred's great-grandson, was the first ruler to be crowned King of all England. Although the concept of national unity was now accepted, the threat from Denmark was not yet over. Seizing power from Ethelred in 1013, the Danish king Swein opened a new chapter in Anglo-Scandinavian relations in which colonization was abandoned in favour of extracting wealth: a vastly expensive tax – the Danegeld – was imposed for this purpose. After Swein's death the throne passed to Cnut (Canute), but following Cnut's demise power returned to the Anglo-Saxon line in the person of Ethelred's son, Edward the Confessor. Edward's reign was one of progress and prosperity – it saw the refoundation of Westminster Abbey – and it was only when he nominated as his successor William of

FIG. 1. THE ALFRED JEWEL, the most precious relic of the Age of King Alfred, presented to the Ashmolean in 1718. It bears the inscription 'ALFRED ORDERED ME TO BE MADE'.

Normandy that unrest began to grow. On Edward's death in 1065 it was not William but Harold, Edward's brother-in law, whom the English acknowledged as their king. In pressing his claim to the throne by force of arms, William was to bring about one of the most comprehensive upheavals in English history.

English society on the eve of the Battle of Hastings was already highly evolved. Urban life had flowered (largely due to Danish influence), providing a focus for commercial activity in the form of markets and military strength in the shape of permanent garrisons. Craftsmen in every material conspired to produce a distinctive and vigorous art style, rivalling any in Europe. Under the Church's influence important centres of scholarship sprang up, notably at Winchester and Canterbury.

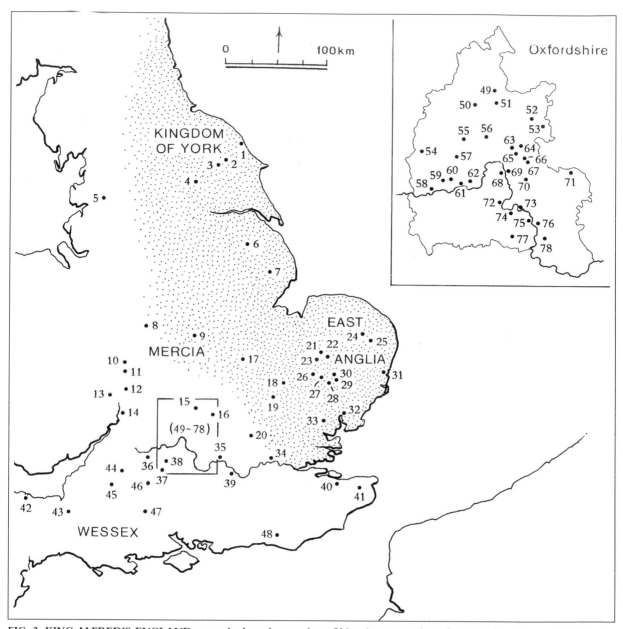

FIG. 2. KING ALFRED'S ENGLAND comprised, at the opening of his reign, a number of separate kingdoms, with Alfred himself ruling over Wessex. The Danelaw (shaded), covering most of the eastern half of England by 902, was gradually regained just in time to fall to the Norman Conquest.

Key to provenances [see inside back cover]: 1 Scarborough, 2 Malton, 3 Scampston, 4 York, 5 Ribble Valley, 6 Owmby, 7 Horncastle, 8 Lichfield, 9 Leicester, 10 Stourbridge, 11 Chaddesley Corbett, 12 Pirton, 13 Malvern, 14 Deerhurst, 15 Brackley, 16 Winslow, 17 Barnwell, 18 Cambridge, 19 Harlton, 20 St.Albans, 21 Brandon, 22 Thetford, 23 Mildenhall, 24 Norwich, 25 Bergh Apton, 26 Icklingham, 27 West Stow, 28 Bury St.Edmunds, 29 Pakenham, 30 Ixworth, 31 Dunwich, 32 Colchester, 33 Coggeshall, 34 London, 35 Marlow, 36 Swindon, 37 Aldbourne, 38 Baydon, 39 Windsor, 40 Faversham, 41 Canterbury, 42 Bossington, 43 Norton Park, 44 Slaughterford, 45 Bradford-on-Avon, 46 Wilcot, 47 Old Sarum, 48 Lewes. Oxfordshire [see inset]: 49 Deddington, 50 Sandford, 51 Middle Aston, 52 Bicester, 53 Blackthorn, 54 Burford, 55 Wilcote, 56 Woodstock, 57 Witney, 58 Radcot, 59 Bampton, 60 Aston, 61 Shifford, 62 Standlake, 63 Islip, 64 Oddington, 65 Woodeaton, 66 Beckley, 67 Woodperry, 68 Osney, 69 Oxford, 70 Horspath, 71 Thame, 72 Abingdon, 73 Dorchester, 74 Long Wittenham, 75 Howbery Park, 76 Crowmarsh, 77 Blewbury, 78 Ipsden

For successes gained in the Conquest William I rewarded his followers with large estates and fortified castles. His generosity was always tempered with self-interest however; the conditions attached to these grants gave the Norman kings an iron grip on the country and transformed the whole face of English society. Lordships were granted on oath of allegiance and carried with them obligations to supply armed knights for the king's armies. A chain of lesser contracts bound every tenant, however small, to the lord and through him to the king. No land-holder escaped this network. A national survey was ordered by William in 1085 to discover the true wealth of England. Officials travelled throughout the land gathering information on economic resources and on property. The immense detail which was contained in the survey, which resulted in the *Domesday Book*, was of great value for the administration of England, although London and the far north were not included.

Two of the Conqueror's sons were to follow him as kings of England. William II (known as Rufus because of his red hair) was written of as stern and avaricious. Having angered the barons and upset the Church, he met a mysterious death while hunting in the New Forest. His younger brother Henry I adopted a more diplomatic approach to political problems but he also shared some of the ruthlessness that characterized the Norman kings. His two legitimate sons were drowned tragically when the 'White Ship' foundered on a journey back from Normandy, leaving England without a male heir; a woman was thought unfit to rule so Henry's daughter Matilda was passed over and in 1135 Stephen, a grandson of William I, succeeded; there followed nineteen years of anarchy until his death. A compromise on the succession was struck with the result that on Stephen's death Matilda's son would become king, ruling as Henry II. So began the line of fourteen Plantagenet monarchs that was to rule over England for more than three hundred years.

FIG. 3. VIKING AGE STIRRUPS of iron with brass wire inlay. Although not a matching pair, they were found together near Magdalen Bridge in Oxford. They may have been lost during a Viking raid in 1009 when the Danes partly burnt the city, or they may derive from a burial.

FIG. 4. VIRGIN AND CHILD, carved in walrus ivory, in a style related to the Winchester School of manuscript illustration of the late tenth or early eleventh century. The panel is thought to have ornamented the cover of a book.

FIG. 5. IVORY CROSIER-HEAD in which the Paschal Lamb stands for the salvation promised to the faithful while the gaping serpent symbolises the jaws of Hell waiting to seize the sinner. This piece was presented to the Ashmolean in 1685, when it was identified as having belonged to Saint Augustine of Hippo. Current opinion places it in the twelfth century, though the mounts are later.

Order was restored and a number of far-reaching legal and constitutional reforms were instituted, many of them based on the latest ideas circulating in the Plantagenet domain in France. Some administrative powers, notably for the regulation of markets and local justice, were devolved to the towns and they (together with the country gentry) began to send representatives to the occasional meetings of the national parliament. In this way an important third force grew up which counterbalanced the powers of king and barons. But it is for his quarrel with Thomas Becket that Henry II is best remembered: this dispute resulted in the murder of Becket on 29 December 1170 at Canterbury Cathedral. The after-effects of this deed were to echo down the centuries, the shrine of the sainted Becket at Canterbury becoming one of the most popular pilgrimage centres in Europe and the inspiration for the first great masterpiece of English literature in the fourteenth century Chaucer's *Canterbury Tales*.

Richard I, Henry's second son succeeded to the throne but spent only about a year of his short reign in England: he was the crusading monarch whose ransom cost the country dear as did his brother John who came to the throne in 1199. When he died seventeen years later England had lost Normandy and most of the empire of Anjou. John also quarrelled with the Church, from which he was excommunicated. These events brought about demands from the barons and in 1215 at Runnymede the King was forced to sign *Magna Carta* (The Great Charter), which re-stated the rights and liberties of both the Church and people.

By 1258, in the reign of Henry III, parliament was meeting regularly and within half a century had won the right to debate all matters concerning the administration of the realm. The nation's wealth had flourished in the meantime. Demand for manufactured goods increased and exports expanded. In the towns powerful craft guilds emerged, regulating the administration of trades. Only the rural peasantry were untouched by this new affluence. Their isolation failed to save them, however, from periodic plagues which swept the country, of which the Black Death of 1348/9 was the most savage.

In military matters too, great changes had been wrought. The role of the mounted knight declined as the country settled into a more orderly internal peace. Under the Platagenets a large militia of freemen was formed, trained in use of the longbow. The united force of cavalry and longbowmen fielded against France during the Hundred Years War (begun in the reign of Edward III) proved devastatingly effective.

By the early fifteenth century life in southern England had settled into a post-feudal mould, although the marcher lords of the north and west still preserved much of their unruly independence. Hardly had Henry IV succeeded to the throne when his rule was challenged by a revolt among the Welsh and a rebellion led by the Earl of Northumberland. Under Henry V the theatre of conflict was carried back to the Continent until the Hundred Years War was brought to a close by a decisive French victory in 1453. Violence and lawlessness were repatriated along with the defeated English mercenaries who, within two years, found ready employment in the opposing factions of the Wars of the Roses. This turbulent period ended with the defeat of Richard III and his forces by Henry VII, founder of the Tudor dynasty.

FIG. 6. GREAT SEAL OF EDWARD III in use 1327-40. The initiator of the Hundred Years War is shown dressed for the fray as leader of the armed forces. He wears a helmet with grated vizor and neck guard, and has his sword chained to his body armour. His surcoat and shield, like the horse's caparison, are charged with the arms of England.

WEAPONS AND WARFARE

War – or the threat of war – was a constant factor throughout the medieval period and the arms and armour from that era reflect the changing methods of warfare and the varying status of the participants. In the Saxon period the carrying of weapons distinguished the free man from the serf. William of Normandy's invasion brought a new type of warrior to English soil and within a few years of the Battle of Hastings the armoured knight on horseback with his mounted retainers had not only proved to be a more efficient fighting unit but was effectively responsible for imposition of the feudal system which permeated society for the next four hundred years. By the fourteenth century the longbow and the pike were to have equally radical effects on the conduct of warfare and the shaping of society.

Before the Conquest every man of the rank of freeman and above would have a spear and a shield whilst the leading warriors would also carry a sword and both might have a *seax* (a short single-edged sword) decorated to a greater or lesser degree according to the rank of the owner. The importance of the sword is evident from the rich fittings found on many of them. The blade had to be strong yet light and flexible, a problem which was solved by pattern-welding – the technique of forging together interwoven strips of iron. Elaboration of the hilt provides the chief evidence for dating. Firstly the pommel, which secured the hilt assembly on the tang and helped balance the sword, offered opportunities for embellishment; then the grip, which might be of wood, antler, horn, metal or of composite structure, had to offer a comfortable hand-hold and might also be decorated; the guard which protected the hand evolved from a simple, functional bar to a wider form whose arms developed into curving decorative quillons, often with expanded terminals providing more scope for decoration.

FIG. 7. THE ABINGDON SWORD's decorated hilt forms one of the most important examples of the Late Saxon silversmith's art. The engraved ornament, inlaid with niello (black silver sulphide), is in the Trewhiddle style of the late ninth century. The guards feature interlacing animal motifs, those on the upper guard seemingly representing the symbols of the Evangelists.

FIG. 8. LATE SAXON AND VIKING SWORDS are characteristically broad-backed (single-edged) with a sharp point, but double-edged blades never entirely lost favour during this period and later they displaced the broad-backed seax during the eleventh century. Knives of Late Saxon date reflect the angular outlines of contemporary swords but generally have no guards. The winged spearhead may also be of tenth-century date.

FIG. 9. PATTERN WELDING. The properties of the constituent strips making up the sword blade were enhanced by repeated working; the many carbon-rich surfaces incorporated into the blade in this way improved its quality. The decorative patterning which resulted on the surface (revealed here by x-rays) was an incidental by-product, but was sometimes enhanced to emphasize the skilled workmanship.

FIG. 10. ARROWHEADS of the early medieval period are characterized by a variety of blade-like forms which, for military purposes were displaced in the course of the thirteenth century by more solid bodkin-like points designed to pierce the plate armour which became more widespread at that time. Similar points were also mounted on crossbow bolts.

The all-purpose single-edged knife, originally plain and functional became more decorative in the medieval period. So did the dagger with its double-edged blade; some dress daggers becoming so elaborate as to be considered fashion accessories rather than weapons of war.

Nowhere else in Europe could the skill of the English longbowman be matched. For three centuries English archers wreaked havoc wherever they served, sending up fearsome barrages of arrows that decimated enemy forces before they could engage at close quarters. The crossbow, which earlier had some use as a hunting weapon, was introduced to the military arsenal by the Normans; by the sixteenth century it had developed into a formidable weapon, shooting bolts that could pass through plate armour.

Widespread adoption of the stirrup, largely under Norman influence, transformed the effectiveness of cavalry. The stirrup welded horse and rider into a stable fighting unit: with legs braced against the stirrup-irons, the rider got a firmer grasp on his lance or sword. A demand for heavier horses arose through the development in the fourteenth century of plate armour, both for man and horse. The elaborately armoured knight, having reached his peak in the fifteenth century, declined shortly afterwards with the development of increasingly efficient firearms. As a result, the whole military system that had characterized the medieval period was profoundly changed and the art of warfare moved on from set-piece tournament-like encounters to the province of the hired mercenary.

FIG. 11. MEDIEVAL SWORDS represented the most impressive (if not the most technologically advanced) products of the swordsmith's craft: the great weapons of the high Middle Ages were massive in construction, reaching as much as 38.5 cm long (centre). Daggers, although always practical, became increasingly decorative: those shown above include a single-edged knife with angular quillons and a shell-like guard, a double-edged stiletto and one with wire decoration around the hilt (fourteenth-century).

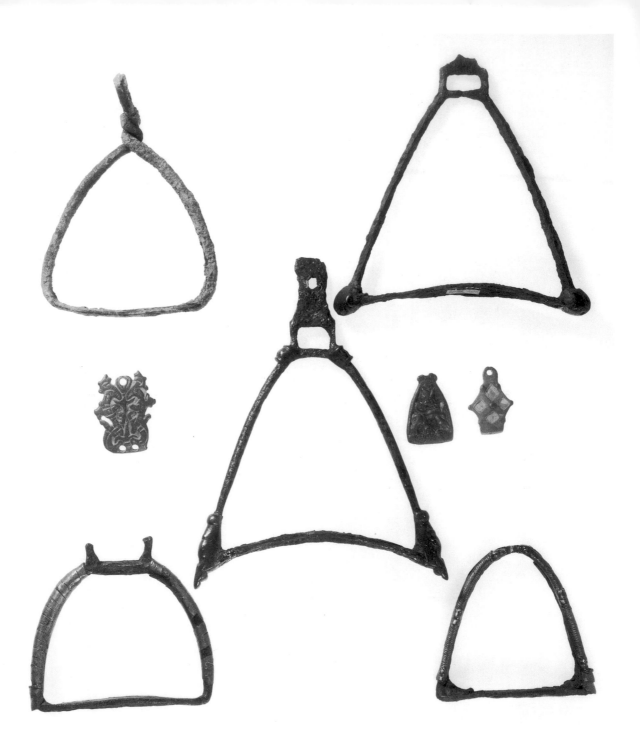

FIG. 12. STIRRUPS. The stirrup was introduced to Great Britain during the ninth century. The earliest types were never decorated but had a twist below the loop which later evolved into a boss. More representative of the type used by the Norman horsemen of the eleventh and twelfth centuries are those with angular frames corresponding in form to some of those depicted in the Bayeux tapestry. A series of decorative mounts has recently been recognized as deriving from the strap-loops of such stirrups: one example in the Ashmolean (centre) incorporates a plate on to which a mount would have been fixed. Other early forms are wrapped with brass strips.

FIG. 13. SPURS. The Viking form of the prick-spur was to play a considerable role in the evolution of early medieval types. It had a simple elongated point and straight arms, though the prick and terminals could vary considerably. Although the Normans introduced their own style the earlier form survived until the mid-twelfth century by which time the spur had begun to develop a curved arm to run under the ankle bone. Major change came with the adoption of the rowel spur in the first half of the fourteenth century. Rowels of the earliest type are small and of six to eight points, though occasionally they were larger, and later the many-pointed wheel-rowel was fashionable. The shank was later increased in length with the adoption of leg armour, the long shank protruding through a slit in the leg-piece. By the fifteenth century this type of spur declined along with the use of heavy armour.

AN EVOLVING ECONOMY

In the reign of Alfred an increasingly effective control of economic affairs is evident from an apparent growth in monetarization as well as from the granting of charters by the Crown. The seeds of this expansion were sown in the seventh century at which time, following two hundred years when only foreign gold coins circulated, mints were established at a number of centres, striking at first in both gold and silver but by 680 producing a single coin – the silver *sceat*. By *c*.780 King Offa of Mercia had established the silver penny which, in size, weight, purity and design remained essentially uniform for centuries.

Although the Viking incursions of 793-866 were catastrophic events in both political and military terms, they also brought unexpected benefits in terms of commercial and urban growth. Against the continuing threat Alfred founded 'burhs', defensive sites which, with growing security, evolved into fortified towns with markets and mints. Each burh issued coins bearing the name of the town and of the moneyer, as well as that of the king. Since control of the mint was exercised by the central authority, the foundations were laid both for efficient control of the money supply and for the development of a decentralized bureaucracy. On occasions when the coinage was changed, local moneyers obtained new dies from London, where they were designed and cut under royal authority. The close relationship between the sovereign and the coinage brought benefits of two kinds: the Crown derived income from duty levied on the production of coin and the sovereign's power was enhanced by the acknowledgement of his authority implicit in all monetary transactions. Two dozen mints were set up during the reign of Athelstan (925-39), by which means the king could coin available bullion more quickly, stimulate local and district commerce, facilitate the collecting of taxes and royal dues, and so effectively maintain his administration and his armed forces at a time when financial support was of the utmost importance. Athelstan assumed the title King of all Britain, which from then on appeared on most of his coins, and instituted a law which laid down that there should be one single coinage.

Evidence from hoards testifies to a Viking thirst for transferable wealth in the form of silver, either in coin or as ingots, hack-silver or ornaments. Along with money raised from captured slaves this booty enabled luxury goods to be bought from as far afield as Russia, Byzantium and Arabia. The Cuerdale hoard, discovered in 1840 by workmen on the embankment of the River Ribble by Cuerdale Hall, near Preston, Lancashire, is the largest hoard of Viking treasure yet found in England. It is not only remarkable for its size but also for the variety of its contents. Buried in a lead-lined chest the hoard contained Anglo-Saxon and Viking coins as well as others from the Middle East, Italy and the Frankish kingdom, in addition to bullion from Ireland and loot from the continent. Except for the ingots much of the silver is fragmentary or cut up but there are very few pieces of waste or manufacturing debris and very few complete objects; it is therefore unlikely that the hoard belonged to a silversmith. An early concern for the quality of silver led to frequent testing of both bullion and coins by

FIG. 14. SCHIST HONES, first appearing in the early phases of Scandinavian settlement, can be traced to a source area in southern Norway. Others of local origin are also common: perhaps they performed complementary functions, the coarse, local stones being used in initial sharpening and those of schist producing a fine cutting edge.

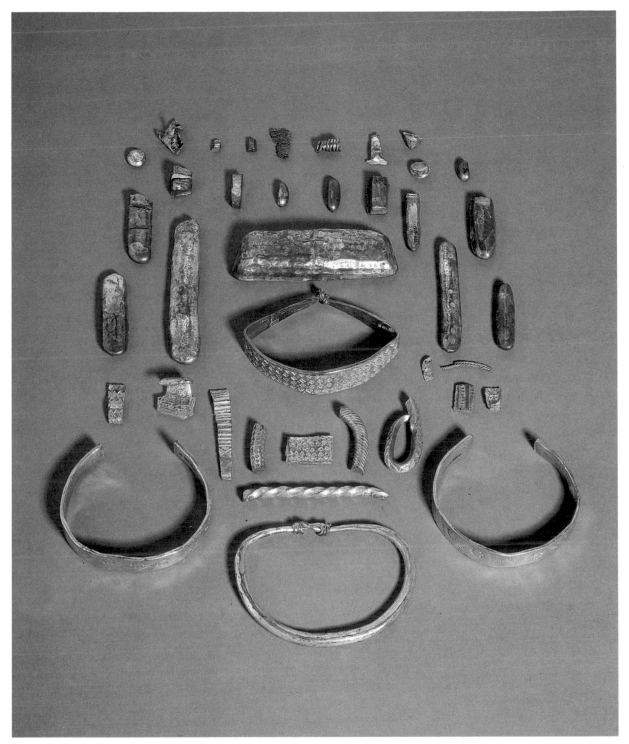

FIG. 15. THE CUERDALE HOARD, discovered in 1840 by workmen on the embankment of the River Ribble by Cuerdale Hall, near Preston, Lancashire, is the largest hoard of Viking treasure yet found in England. It had been buried in a leaden chest which contained over 8,500 pieces of silver, weighing some 40 kg: it included about 7,500 coins and 1,000 ingots, ornaments and cut fragments of silver. The treasure contained Anglo-Saxon and Viking coins as well as others from the Middle East, Italy and the Frankish kingdom, in addition to bullion from Ireland and loot from the Continent. Coins dating to AD 901-5 give a terminal date for the find. Further elements of the hoard are held in Liverpool (National Museum & Galleries on Merseyside) and in London (The British Museum).

FIG. 16. PENNY OF ATHELSTAN (925-39): the obverse bears the King's name and the inscription REX TOT[IUS] BRIT[ANNICUS] 'King of all Britain'; on the reverse is the name of the moneyer, MAETHELWEALD, and that of the mint, OX[ONIENSIS] VRB[S] – the City of Oxford.

FIG. 17. GOLD NOBLE, the most notable English gold coin of the late Middle Ages, introduced in 1344 by Edward III was virtually pure gold – 99.5% fine and worth 6s.8d. On the obverse the king is seen aboard a ship holding a sword aloft and defending himself with a shield, emblazoned with the quartered arms of England and France – both a display of national pride and an announcement of royal ambitions.

pecking the surface or nicking the edge. Ingots formed a practical means of storing large amounts of silver and could be easily divided and used as currency. Coins dating to 901-5 give a terminal date for the find.

The eventual settlement of the Danelaw seems not to have altered the trading tendencies of the Vikings; coins were struck there, sometimes copying those issued by the king in the south. At York, the capital of the Danelaw, archaeological and historical evidence combine to demonstrate the city's status as a major commercial clearing-house for the entire north-east of England: merchants traded in silk, amber, walrus ivory and furs, as well as more utilitarian items such as schist hones from Norway, which came to form the basis of an extensive trade across the North Sea, surviving well into the early medieval period.

By the thirteenth century England's wealth lay in her wool trade. In 1275 Edward I levied a tax of seven shillings and sixpence on every sack of wool exported. The already-prosperous wool merchants consented but considered a higher tax demand of forty shillings a sack in the last decade of the century as an 'evil exaction'. The fact that the king felt able to demand such a large sum demonstrates the importance of the wool trade to the economy in Edward I's reign. Edward, a great statesman and an able administrator turned his attention to reforming the coinage which had deteriorated through wear and clipping. The introduction in 1279 of a new coinage, which consisted of pennies, halfpennies, farthings and a new denomination the groat worth four pence, testifies to not only a strong administration but a growing economy. The new halfpenny and farthing also did away with the annoying necessity of halving and quartering whole coins.

A costly war with France in the first half of Edward III's reign (1327-77) caused adverse economic conditions to which were added the appalling consequences of the Black Death. When the war with France was finally ended in 1360 the treaty settlement gave Edward some worthwhile economic advantages. He relinquished his claim to the French throne in return for extensive possessions in the wine-growing regions of the south and a base at the port of Calais. England's major post-war effort lay in the restoration of her wool-trade. Further export taxes were levied on wool, a move which brought about some decline in the market for English wool on the Continent. On the other hand, it proved of benefit to English clothiers since the costs of their raw materials were now lower than those faced by foreign competitors and the consequent growth of the English cloth industry helped restore the balance of trade. The Crown kept control of the cloth industry through the alnager, an officer whose role it was to inspect the bales of cloth for quality, length, weight and breadth and to apply his seal to them if they proved of marketable standard; without an alnage seal the cloth could not legally be sold; the earliest examples so far known are attributed to the 1380s. However the country's wealth was ensured through continuing exports of raw wool and of cloth through the staple towns, especially Calais, one consequence of this being the establishment of a mint there in 1363 where an important new gold coin was struck. The use of gold in coinage had been spreading throughout Europe for some time and in order to further commercial activity, especially with major customers like the Flemish merchants, Edward III was obliged to conform. After a brief unsuccessful first attempt an effective gold coin was introduced in

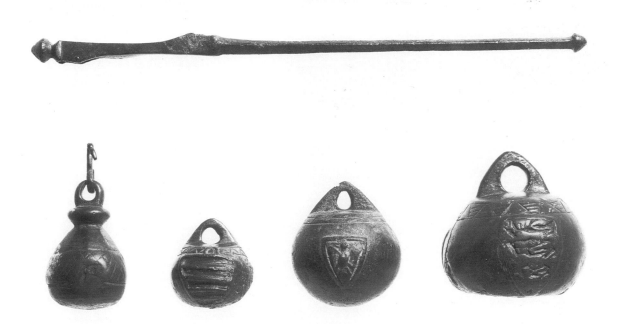

FIG. 18. STEELYARDS were re-introduced to Britain during the medieval period (their earlier use having ended with the Roman period). Moveable counterweights are more commonly found than the balance arm. These weights are made with a lead core enclosed by a bronze casing, the latter often bearing heraldry associated with Richard Earl of Cornwall and Poitou indicating the latter's authority to issue weights on behalf of the monarch.

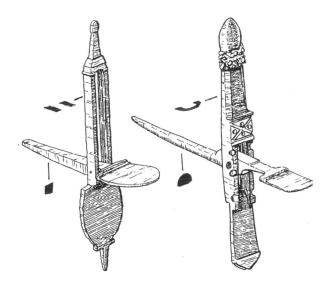

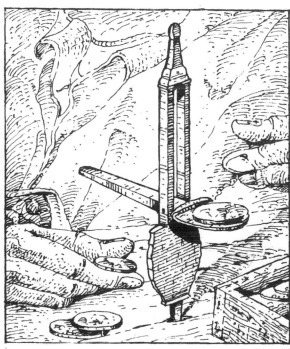

FIG. 19. TUMBRELS were designed for weighing a particular coin against the fixed theoretical weight; light coins would not lift the weighted arm whereas those of good weight would balance the arm. Their use was restricted to mint officials by Edward I in 1292, since overweight coins could be identified and 'clipped' of their excess metal.

FIG. 20. The tumbrel in use.

FIG. 21. PARROT-BEAKED JUG, whose form, fabric and face-mask decoration all show it to be a local Oxfordshire product although influenced by imported French wares which arrived in England in the wake of the wine trade.

1344 – the noble, worth one third of a pound or 6s. 8d., an especially beautiful issue being Calais. Until the loss of Calais in 1558, control of the wool trade remained a powerful political weapon.

As the economy expanded it was the duty of governments to protect the citizens in their dealings both in national and international commerce. The State guaranteed that coins issued in the name of the King were of the specific weight and quality of silver laid down by monetary law. Accurate weighing therefore became particularly important and governments began to concern themselves with supervising weights and scales and also measures of capacity and length. Early systems were based on natural standards which were inevitably imprecise – grains (of wheat) for weighing, (human) feet for measuring length. The Anglo-Saxon measures were preserved by William I; the Doomsday survey records land holdings in Anglo-Saxon hides, acres, roods and perches. Cloth was measured in cubits of two feet, the customary width being two cubits (one elne/ell). The imprecision which surrounded these measures was progressively limited by statutory controls introduced by Richard I and Edward I, providing for the creation of official metal standards against which copies were verified before being distributed. Despite repeated restatements of the principle that there should be but one system of weights and measures, six different standards have been recognized for the pound at different times. While many of the early terms survived, the history of weights and measures in the medieval and later period is one of progressive refinement and standardization. The citizen was thus protected in everyday dealings and international commerce benefitted from the confidence engendered by a uniform system.

A healthy, growing economy can be recognized by its ability to generate surpluses that can be used to acquire luxury goods. An expansion of imports of this kind can be detected in the fourteenth century when English society, perhaps influenced by the culture of the French during the Thirty Years War became more sophisticated. This too was the age of chivalry when attention was paid to increasing pomp and display in buildings, in clothing and in elaborate tournaments. Edward III founded the Order of the Garter; his son the Black Prince was the epitome of medieval chivalry. Wine was imported from Gascony and seemingly connected with this trade are the pottery 'parrot-beak' jugs of French manufacture which have been found, for example, in the medieval port of Southampton. By 1453 England had lost its influence in this region of France and as a result trade declined, which meant that England was no longer supplied with Gascon wine and an important market for English wheat and cloth, was lost.

Among the peasantry there was great diversity between those who remained unfree but gave labour service to their lord for the use of land and those who began to pay rent out of earnings. More husbandmen began to be hired for wages which, although low, meant that more money was in circulation. Even this small economic freedom for the low-waged had its adverse side. A new government poll tax in 1381 was so unpopular that it resulted in the Peasants' Revolt. In an economy in which the highest denomination was, for many centuries, the silver penny there were drawbacks at the lower end of the market where consumers frequently found that they required smaller units of change. Even halfpennies and farthings were of too high a denomination for many purchases and in some places monetary tokens cast in lead were used. A number of moulds for tokens of this type have been excavated and the suggestion has been made that they may be associated with taverns. With the cost of a gallon of beer in the thirteenth century at one penny, it is evident that the use of tokens was almost essential in order that the thirsty customer could buy a pint of his favourite drink.

FIG. 22. TOKEN MOULD of slate, on one side of which are engraved four circlets, one incomplete: that at the top is a human figure, the next has a male head, the third a backward-looking animal and the last dotted squares.

19

AGRARIAN ECONOMY

Until the late eighteenth century England was essentially a rural society, with the majority of the population gaining a living from the land. The urban populace was small, and much industrial activity was carried out on a small scale in rural areas and on a localized basis.

Following the Norman Conquest the basic economic unit became the manor, a property owned or held by a single lord and managed from one administrative centre. Rents, in cash, kind or service, were paid to the lord of the manor for tenure and use of manorial lands and homes, and for most people the manor court provided the sole point of contact with the legal system. From the fifteenth century onwards the importance of the manor declined, but control by the land-owner over rents and wages continued largely unchallenged until the 1830s.

A key feature of the agricultural system in the Middle Ages lay in the strip-farming system. Land under cultivation was generally divided into three

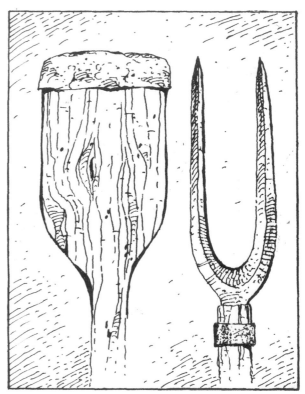

FIG. 24. SPADE-SHOES of iron turned wooden spades into useful implements at comparatively low cost, at a time when implements of solid metal would have been prohibitively expensive. Iron pitch-forks were introduced in the medieval period, although others entirely of wood survived in use until the nineteenth century.

FIG. 23. TITHE BARNS or granges, like this one at Bredon, (Hereford & Worcester) were built by landlords – especially the ecclesiastical authorities – to store the grain they received as taxes. (Photograph : John Steane)

large, open fields, of which two would be used for arable crops and one left fallow in rotation for grazing. Each field was then parcelled out in unfenced strips, for which rent or labour services were due. The ridge-and-furrow topography characteristic of medieval field systems is a common feature of the present-day landscape but evidence from tools is scarce: wooden elements such as handles have generally decayed while the remains of iron fittings (which were in any case comparatively rare) often survive only in a corroded and fragmentary condition. Wealthy land-owners began increasingly to encroach on common land for cultivation in the thirteenth century and the continuing enclosure of these open fields remained a contentious issue between land-owner and tenant farmer for many centuries to come.

FIG. 25. WOOL WEIGHTS were developed to help control the trade in (and tax on) this all-important commodity. Official 'tronators' toured the wool markets to see that due customs duty was paid; each officer carried a pair of weights for weighing out the wool on the common balances which occupied the market place.

At the heart of England's rural economy lay the wool trade. Although centrally administered it was, for the countryman, a cottage industry with the shearer passing the raw wool to the spinner (usually a woman) and, if it was to be woven into cloth, eventually to the weaver. Middlemen collected wool to be exported, but if it was to be made into cloth then many more processes were completed locally. These ranged from carding, in which the wool was teased out, a process initially involving a hand-held comb but which by the early fourteenth century was carried out on boards set with iron teeth, to fulling, in which the woven cloth was trampled in a tub of fuller's earth to degrease and shrink it; by the end of the medieval period the latter process was aided by water-driven fulling mills. Entire villages might be employed at every stage of the wool trade from breeding the sheep to production of the cloth.

FIG. 26. LARGE SHEARS, used in clipping sheep, changed little in design from the Middle Ages until the present century. Smaller varieties made of iron were replaced for domestic purposes by scissors from about 1300 onwards. Shears of bronze with inset iron cutting-edges were used in cloth-finishing

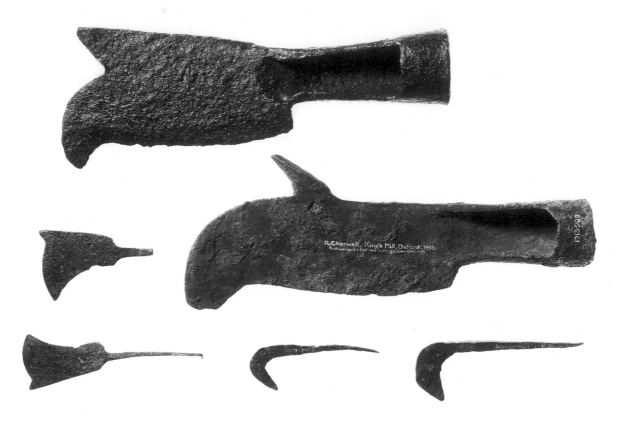

FIG. 27. BILL-HOOKS. The larger ones were used in wood management while the smaller pruning hooks were purely domestic implements. Conservatism in implement forms makes precise dating difficult.

FIG. 28. MILK BOWL or dish from Dean Court Farm, Oxford, a grange of Abingdon Abbey, where excavations revealed a marked interest in dairy farming in the twelfth and thirteenth century. Such bowls were used in the separating process when cream was skimmed off to be used to make butter.

Woodland also played a vital part in the economy, although (on the evidence of *Domesday Book*) by the mid-eleventh century it covered only about 15% of the English countryside. Its valuable resources were categorized respectively as timber, wood and firewood. Timber, from the biggest trees, was essential for all types of building as well as for wagons and ships; wood came from that part of the forest which had been coppiced and was useful for poles, hurdles, fencing and faggots, as well as smaller objects like tools and besoms, which were made in the woods themselves; finally the forest floor yielded the dead wood suitable for burning as fuel. Woodland had to be managed so that areas to be coppiced were given the appropriate amount of growing-time to produce the required thicknesses of wood. The essential tree-pruning instrument used in coppicing, hedging and the maintenance of orchards, was the bill-hook. Mounted on long wooden shafts they also made fearsome weapons, giving rise to the companies of 'bill-men' that formed a common element in the English country militia. As a source of food the wooded areas were important to

FIG. 29. NET-SINKERS of oolitic limestone have been found in some numbers in the Oxford region, notably from the Thames and its immediate surroundings. They are thought to have been used in the freshwater fishery which formed a significant element in the medieval subsistence economy.

the countryman but to the Crown certain forests were reserved for sport and for the preservation of royal deer. These royal forests, large tracts of territory which included farmland, villages and even towns as well as the areas of woodland pasture where the deer were protected, were governed by special laws which led to much discontent between the monarch and his subjects.

Smaller woods too were a source of revenue to owners, who might rent them out or sell the products. Woods were divided into coppices, sometimes parted by ditches or by banks topped by fences. Some coppices were planted for specific purposes: hornbeam was valued for the cogs of waterwheels, hazel for wattle. Oak trees were normally left to grow to full height and the bark of the mature tree was utilized by tanners. The woodland was also used as pannage for pigs and as pasture for beasts. Under the care of the swineherd, pigs were allowed to feed on fallen beech nuts, hazel nuts and acorns. Foliage was also used as cattle feed. As well as firewood for the home, faggots supplied fuel to fire pottery kilns in some areas and to produce charcoal in others.

Fishing formed an important element in the medieval economy, since fresh fish compensated for the lack of meat during the winter months and formed an important part of the diet at a time when religious fasts were widely observed. Inland, riparian owners (owners of lakes and river banks) generally had a monopoly on fishing rights, although poaching was widespread. There were strict laws governing the building of weirs, a major device used in river fishing. Ponds or 'stews' were also contrived in which fish were farmed in captivity. Wildfowl were extensively hunted and swans were husbanded for their meat.

Off-shore, both nets and lines were used in fishing and certain towns became especially associated with fishing; Yarmouth was famous for herring, Rye and Winchelsea for plaice and whiting, Scarborough and Grimsby for cod. As early as the fifteenth century, fishing vessels were venturing into Icelandic waters, bringing the fish back alive in wells in the hold. Oysters, whelks and mussels were also widely harvested, with oysters becoming increasingly a food of the rich from the 1500s onwards.

INDUSTRY

Throughout the Middle Ages, production of most goods lay in the hands of craftsmen operating their own workshops within towns. From *c.*1130 onwards guilds were established, initially for craftsmen but later also for merchants. Craft guilds were formed for the mutual benefit of their members. They set standards for the quality of products and for professional behaviour; they also regulated apprenticeships, which lasted no fewer than seven and sometimes as many as ten years. Not all crafts had guilds and neither did they want them: whilst internal control by a guild might be beneficial to both craftsmen and customers, externally imposed levies brought financial burdens on the members. Each was taxed locally for the right to take up the freedom of the town – a necessity if they were to practise their craft and sell their products within it: charges ranged from quite small sums in the case of those who followed their fathers as freemen, to more substantial fees for those who had been apprenticed to a freeman. 'Foreigners' (that is anyone not local) had to prove their skill and pay a considerable sum for rights of citizenship as a member of the guild. Then too, guilds paid fees to the Crown in order to gain licences by royal charter. Guild members usually held the monopoly on their trade within most towns, though this was generally not the case in London.

The quality control practised by the guild was particularly important when the task in hand required the skill of more than one craft, or when totally different crafts combined to complete the finished article. In the leather trade, for example, there were distinct guilds for the skinners and for several of those who prepared the leather and who produced the finished goods. Tanners worked only with cattle skins, and the curing of these was a long process; tawyers processed the skins of other animals producing a much softer leather popular with glovers. Curriers finished the skins, trimming and cutting to the thickness required. Cordwainers made new shoes from leather, while cobblers mended or re-made old ones; other consumers of leather included those who made budgets or bags, costrels or bottles, black-jacks or jugs, and harness for horses. Amongst the latter, the saddlers of London, for example, were in almost constant dispute with the loriners, who made horse-bits and other metal items for harness, and with the joiners who made the wooden saddle-trees. Similarly, the cutlers, who

finished, assembled and sold knives, had to take responsibility for the work of their suppliers, who included the bladesmiths, hafters and sheathers. Many craftsmen and guilds adopted stamps or marks to show that work was up to standard, although these were quite often forged.

There were numerous guilds for metal workers, ranging from those who specialized in particular metals such as the goldsmiths, silver-smiths and pewterers, while others such as the bell-founders, armourers and loriners were aligned on particular products. In rural areas the village smith would produce a range of objects from horseshoes and nails to agricultural implements and architectural metalwork. With the progressive growth of towns increasing specialization became both possible and desirable, so that by 1422 in London the number of iron-working guilds had risen to fourteen.

By that time the lockyers, for example, were listed as a separate guild, when at an earlier period locks and keys would have been made by the blacksmith. It was not until the eleventh century that locks became widely used in England.

Of all the workers in metal the goldsmith had perhaps the most critical importance for the Crown. Both the Minster Lovell Jewel and the Alfred Jewel have left us an inheritance of supreme Anglo-Saxon goldsmith's skills, incorporating filigree, granulation, chasing, engraving and enamelling. More important however was the fact that in the Middle Ages silver was used almost exclusively as the principal metal of the coinage until the reign of Edward III (1327-77). Henry III (1216-72) by ordinance in 1238 set standards for gold and silver articles but it was not until 1300 in the reign of Edward I that a statute was passed requiring not only that all silver articles were to be of the sterling standard, the same as coinage at 92.5% pure, but also that they were to be assayed by the warden of the Goldsmiths' Company and marked with a leopard's head before they could be sold. The goldsmith's workshop would have been responsible for embellishing expensive items with enamel work. Enamelling was at a developed stage in the Middle Ages, when three principal techniques were practised. Cloisonné work is the art of enamelling within cells produced by soldering wires or thin strips on a base-plate; once the cells were filled with powdered enamel (glass) the piece was fired

FIG. 30. HORSESHOES occur in Britain in contexts as early as ninth and tenth centuries. Their prior use remains a matter of debate. The earliest shown here are of Norman type: the nail holes have deep oval or rectangular counter-sinkings which push out the edge of the shoe to produce a typical wavy profile. Calkins moulded on the heels are a regular feature. Horseshoes of wider and heavier form appear during the fourteenth century, when the wavy outline disappears. This type of shoe remains virtually unchanged until the seventeenth century.

at between 700 and 800°C and finally the enamel surface was polished smooth. The champlevé technique involves the cutting of the metal surface to form a depression; the enamel is placed into the depression, fired and polished. Basse-taille, a development of the champlevé technique was invented in the late thirteenth century; here the enamels were translucent rather than opaque. As it was the only method available of imparting permanent colour to metal, enamelling was particularly popular in the production of small, decorative objects like brooches and horse-trappings, especially as colour was indispensable in depicting heraldry. These less valuable objects were produced by a variety of bronze-founders.

The cutters of dies and makers of moulds were as vital to many craftsmen as were tool-makers. Stone moulds served in the production of ingots, ornaments, tokens, etc., in copper and lead alloy and effectively permitted a rudimentary form of mass-production. Moulds could also be of bronze or brass, potter's clay

or fine-grained limestone. Crucibles of fired clay were used in a range of metal-working and glass-working processes. The forms of these simple vessels varied little over the centuries, making precise dating on formal grounds rather difficult.

The glass-manufacturers were dependent on mould-makers (who supplied crucibles) and on metalsmiths for tools, but their industry most of all required large amounts of wood to fuel the furnaces. Glass was made from sand and wood-ash (usually beech), while various metal oxides were added to produce different colours. The requirements for glass production meant that glass houses were situated in woodland sites within reach of a source of sand: the Weald of Surrey and Sussex was probably the most important English centre of the craft in medieval times.

Reference has already been made to the importance of wool production in the agricultural economy and also to the woollen trade as the principal source of wealth in England in the Middle Ages. Sheep were

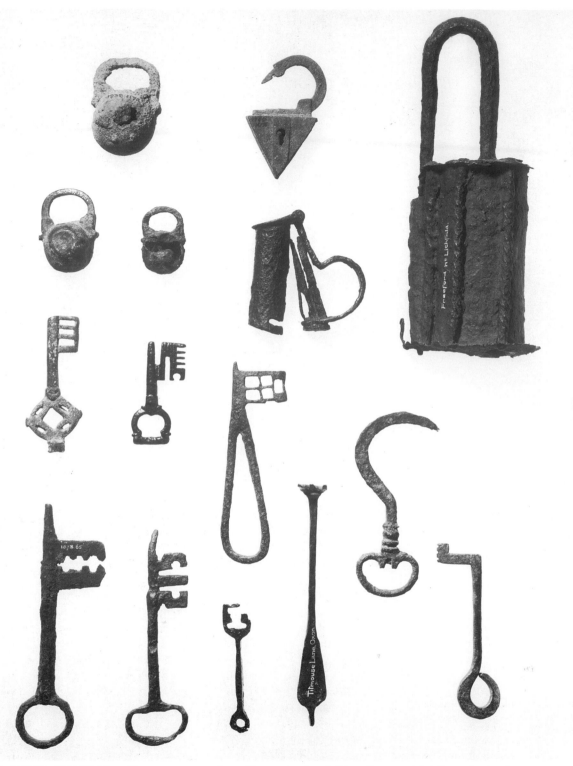

FIG. 31. LOCKS AND KEYS testify to a preoccupation with security. Latch-lifters (bottom right) form the simplest group. In barrel locks (current from the Late Saxon period to the late Middle Ages) the loop or shackle is held secure by a spring catch within a closed cylinder; the key is inserted through the base or the side of the lock and slides up the hasp, compressing the spring and so releasing the lock. Simple mortice locks are known from around the time of the Conquest: from an early date they were warded, that is to say, fitted with stops corresponding to the pattern of clefts on a particular key.

FIG. 32. LATE SAXON GOLDWORK illustrating the skill of native goldsmiths. The inscription on one reading IN XPO NOMEN CHLLA FIC (In Christ my name has been made Culla), suggests that it may be a baptismal or investiture ring. On another double-headed snakes entwine with vine stems, which may once have had a gem as a centre-piece. The bezel of a third ring is formed by two intertwined snakes biting their own bodies. Interlacing snakes again feature on the gold filigree ornament of a base-silver sword pommel found at Windsor (top).

FIG. 33. ENAMELLING, having declined under the Anglo-Saxons, enjoyed a revival in the early medieval period, although the art was never lost in England. Shown here are two decorative discs, an annular heraldic brooch, two square Viking age brooches, two heraldic harness pendants and a stirrup mount.

FIG. 34. CRUCIBLES were essential items for melting a variety of precious and base metals prior to casting; they were also used in glass working. One-piece moulds might be employed in casting ingots or for items with detail on one face only; two-piece moulds were essential for double-sided castings. Complex items were cast by the lost wax method, in non-reusable clay moulds.

reared in most parts of the country, giving a range of wools. Until the spinning wheel was introduced towards the end of the thirteenth century, spinning was carried out with a free-hanging spindle weighted with a whorl of stone, bone, pottery or some other material. In the medieval period weaving was at first a domestic craft carried out by women but by the end of the eleventh century male workers had taken over the production of cloth. By the middle of the twelfth century the industry had expanded in certain centres so that guilds of weavers had established themselves in London, Winchester, Lincoln, Oxford, Huntingdon and Nottingham. Until the eleventh century the upright loom was used: clay weights held the warp in tension while heddle rods were tied to the warp threads, by which means they could be raised to form the shed. When the horizontal loom was adopted, and later when the use of treadles was developed, the process was much speeded up. The width of cloth was restricted by the size of the loom and that in turn was determined by the comfortable range for the weaver to pass the shuttle through the shed. A two-man horizontal loom was later introduced, providing the

broadcloth which was to become a sought-after English textile. Fullers were the next craft to deal with the cloth by trampling it in a tub of fuller's earth to remove the grease: fulling shrinks the cloth, makes it matt and gives it a softer finish. This craft too became more mechanized with the use of water-driven hammers to beat the cloth and fulling mills became established in rural districts near suitable sources of water. Then it was the turn of the dyers (though dyeing could be carried out before or after weaving). Most dyes were of vegetable origin. The dyers had to be near a plentiful supply of water and a place to dispose of the waste they generated. Finally the cloth was checked by an officer called the alnager and from the fourteenth century we have evidence of alnage tax having been paid in the form of lead seals which were attached to the approved length of cloth. These seals may show size, weight and place of origin, while others were later added to record the dyestuffs used.

The pottery industry in England was highly organized by the end of the Roman period but became completely fragmented during the early Anglo-Saxon period when only coarse hand-made wares were produced. Whenever wood and clay were freely available local potters could always supply their own communities, but for a full-scale industry to evolve certain developments were necessary. Improvements came in the late seventh century with the adoption of the slow turntable, rotated by hand; first noted in the Ipswich area, its use later became widespread. More developed industries gradually evolved and the fast wheel is known from the mid ninth century. Three principal types are most commonly found, each named after the site where it was first identified. St. Neots type wares are characterized by a shell-filled body whose softness and uneven firing indicate the use of a simple clamp kiln; Thetford type wares are of hard grey fabric with sand temper, while Stamford type wares have a distinctive white or buff fabric fired in oxidising conditions, contrasting with the darker reduced wares of East Anglia. The Stamford potters were the first in England to make use of lead glazes which generally fired to a pale yellow or green and were applied sparingly to spouted pitchers and to jugs. English potters, having survived the upheavals of the Norman Conquest with little change to their output and despite some set-backs in the twelfth century, had developed by the fourteenth century a successful and technically efficient industry, which produced predominantly green-glazed jugs and plain cooking pots. The medieval potter, however, was held in no very high regard: nowhere in England was even the most modest guild of potters formed to rival those of the blacksmiths, coppersmiths, woodworkers and leatherworkers whose products in the form of cooking-pots, tablewares and other vessels far out-priced those of common clay. There is evidence to suggest that some potters practised their craft on a semi-professional basis throughout the medieval period and that proportion seems actually to have increased when far-reaching changes in the character of the pottery industry can be detected, no doubt reflecting wide social upheavals. Notwithstanding their lowly status and innate conservatism, potters gradually increased their range of products. In the fourteenth century growing affluence led to increasing numbers of metal cooking-pots in circulation which in turn led the potters to diversify into more elaborate decorative jugs and cheap copies of metal forms.

FIG. 35. SPINNING and weaving equipment was technologically very simple in early medieval England: annular loom-weights of clay, spindle-whorls in various materials and bone beaters had remained largely unchanged since the arrival of the Anglo-Saxons. Changes were wrought with the introduction of the spinning wheel and the horizontal loom, though these are as yet little represented archaeologically.

FIG. 36. COOKING-POTS and storage vessels were invariably unglazed in the medieval period. Lids are virtually unknown from this time, although wooden covers would have kept out vermin and discs of stone found in medieval contexts have been similarly interpreted. Vessels for holding liquids were sometimes provided with a spout or with a bung-hole for a stopper or spigot.

FIG. 37. JUGS were commonly glazed, although often sparingly. Only the external surface was glazed during the medieval period: given the toxic nature of lead glaze, this was probably a prudent practice. Large jugs with globular bodies and surprisingly thin walls are common; more cylindrical balluster jugs were an Oxford speciality. Applied ornament as well as glaze is common.

SOCIAL EVOLUTION

Major changes in political, religious or economic affairs may have had little impact on day-to-day life in the lower echelons of society, but a place of shelter and food to eat were of universal relevance.

Housing reflected the wide social divisions which marked early medieval society. Fortified castles, which sheltered the Norman nobility gave way to the more domestic moated manor house as internal tensions lessened, while at the other end of the social scale the peasant's hovel changed little. On the other hand, the homes of the urban merchant classes developed strikingly, along with the rising fortunes of their owners.

From the Late Saxon period until the latter half of the sixteenth century, timber was the building medium which predominated from the aisled hall of the nobleman to the peasant's hut. Barns, mills and even the majority of defensive structures were similarly constructed; only in the more important ecclesiastical buildings was masonry common (and even then belfries and roofs were made of wood), while in the poorer structures wattle-and-daub filled out the walls. The typical dwelling which emerged after the Conquest had but two rooms: a larger living room in which all public activity took place, with a smaller private 'bower' leading off it. Both chambers were open to the high-pitched roof where smoke from a central hearth collected and filtered out. When stone came to be more widely employed it was used primarily to build a strong ground-floor chamber, which served for storage, while the dwelling space was moved to the first floor, an arrangement that particularly recommended itself to the rising merchant class since it combined premises suitable for both business and domestic use. A third and larger form of building perpetuated the late Saxon type of hall with aisles at either side. In wealthier households the screens which were commonly erected to shelter the hall from draughts became formalized into a 'screens passage', cutting off the end containing the entrance. As various additional elements began to take on separate identities – kitchen (often an outside detached building). pantry, buttery, etc. – their entrances all led into the screens passage, which became a standard feature. In this form the hall itself might still have a central open hearth but from the sixteenth century wall-mounted fireplaces had an important effect on the development of the hall, rendering the high open roof unnecessary.

Many halls now had an additional floor inserted, the low ceiling (often with moulded ornament) lending a more intimate atmosphere while the floor above provided extra sleeping space. By this time stone had become the normal building material for the very best houses and was also used for cottages in areas where local stone was plentiful but in other places timber-framed houses were the norm. The technique of timber framing had in the meantime reached its peak, again showing regional variations. Brickwork, which hitherto had been used exclusively for details, now became the normal medium for filling-out timber framing; entire houses of brick became increasingly common.

Certainly geographical location would have influenced the choice of materials used in building but in

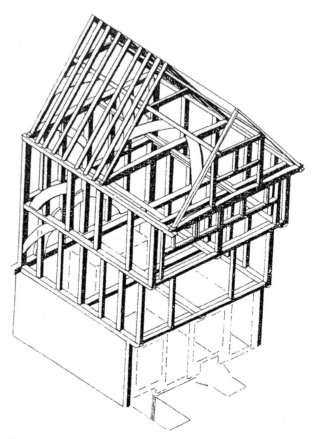

FIG. 38. LATE MEDIEVAL HOUSE at 126 High Street, Oxford. Only the ground floor and cellar have stone walls; the upper floors are timber framed, each projecting beyond the other to provide maximum floor space. Surveyed and drawn by Julian Munby.

FIG. 39. FLOOR TILES, inlaid with a great variety of designs, range from the highly intricate to bold, rough outlines. Ornament was applied in several ways: on monochrome tiles the pattern might be formed in relief, either glazed or unglazed. In the second quarter of the thirteenth century a new type of decoration was introduced: the tiler stamped the decoration into the clay and filled the cavities with white slip to produce a two-colour tile. Subsequent glazing transformed the slip to a warm honey colour. Heraldic themes are common, and patterns frequently spread over several tiles which combine to complete the design.

the early period most roofs were thatched, wooden shingles being a less common alternative. Stone slates which had been used by the Romans were too heavy for wooden Saxon buildings but by the fourteenth century, in order to reduce the frequency of fires, stone and slate tiles began to be used for private houses, when it could be afforded, as well as for public buildings. Indeed as early as 1212 in London an ordinance was issued by which no roofs were to be covered with reed, sedge, straw or stubble but only with tile, shingle, boards or plastered straw. Tile-making spread throughout most of eastern and south-eastern England before the end of the thirteenth century. Bricks and tiles were also used for paving but evidence from invoices and bills indicates that the tiles introduced to make patterned floors were of a different quality and much more expensive. Patterned and glazed floor tiles first began to be used widely in England during the thirteenth century. Henry III almost certainly brought tile-makers over from France to work on the floors of the royal palaces. The French

tilers taught their techniques to English craftsmen, many of whom may already have been making plain roof-tiles, and the use of decorated paving tiles became increasingly widespread in royal and noble houses. The late fifteenth century saw tiles being more commonly laid in the homes of the wealthy merchant classes. Tiles of medieval type fell from fashion during the sixteenth century as changes in taste brought into favour Italianate paved floors, generally in black and white.

Lighting in the dark medieval house was very basic, the simplest form being the rush or taper. Lamps were originally open dishes with oil, made either of stone or pottery, the latter of a single-shell type but from the thirteenth century developing a double-shelled form designed to catch the drips. Hanging lamps or 'cruiscs' of wrought iron although more complex in design, operated on the same principle. Candles provided an alternative means of lighting; these were made by dipping repeatedly a wick of rush or cloth into molten beeswax or fat which had been saved in the kitchen.

FIG. 40. LAMPS of the simplest form have a single container for the oil but from the thirteenth century onward were commonly made with double shells, which helped to catch drips. These were an Oxfordshire speciality.

Among the many developments that can be traced between the end of the Anglo-Saxon period and the Tudor age, those that took place in the kitchen were slower than most. It was not until the nineteenth century that alternatives to cooking over an open fire were available in the average home and the fuel burned was mostly wood and peat. At the beginning of this period only the most privileged would have had an area inside the dwelling house which could be called the kitchen, most cooking taking place outside of the living quarters. From being a detached building the kitchen gradually became an integral part of the main dwelling, fully so by the fifteenth or sixteenth century.

The range of techniques available to the medieval cook was quite considerable. In well-off households the cuisine could be elaborate even by today's standards. The poor were denied access to many of the more exotic ingredients, but imaginative use was made of a wide range of naturally occurring plants which helped to add variety and piquancy to the diet while feast days allowed a rare opportunity to break with a fare of very restricted range. Cereals such as barley, oats and rye formed the basis of the average diet, cooked in the form of thick broths or 'pottages' and enriched with vegetables, meat or fish according to availability. Bread provided the other principal source of sustenance, most commonly in the form of simple hearth-cakes, for ovens were as yet unfamiliar in ordinary houses. They were most commonly to be found in manor houses and monasteries, and poorer folk might take their bread or meat for roasting in these ovens or in those of professional bakers who began to appear at this time; payment was made in cash or with a portion of the food.

The popular image of a rustic society dining off spit-roasted oxen and haunches of venison is far from the reality of everyday life in medieval England. Although meat was the basis of a noble diet, vegetables offered some variation and native herbs and aromatic plants were augmented after the Conquest, when recipes were improved by a variety of exotic spices, many of them originating in the Arab world. Sugar made its appearance at this time, but remained a luxury commodity for several centuries. Fish formed a useful source of protein for those who could get it and meatless days dictated by religious practice increased the demand. Rabbits (first introduced in controlled warrens by the Normans but quickly established in the wild) and hares were the principal game animals of the peasant. The fortunate nobleman might dine on venison, but deer hunting was a jealously guarded privilege with stringent penalties to discourage illegal poaching. Sauces complemented the flavour of meat and fish dishes as well as disguising the taste of flesh which was all too often tainted through lack of adequate cool storage.

Milk from sheep as well as cows was the universal liquid food. Ale was more widely appreciated and was drunk at all hours of the day and by all levels of society. There were plenty of small brewhouses but every major household had its own brewhouse and a range of strengths was produced from the weakest 'small ales' given to children to full-bodied barley malt. The technique of brewing with hops, introduced from the Continent in the fourteenth century, produced beer which was superior in taste and keeping properties. Cider making came from Normandy in the twelfth century while mead, the drink of the Anglo-Saxon aristocracy, was gradually eclipsed by imported sweet wines. English wine-growing declined in the face of cheap and plentiful imports from Gascony under Henry II and perhaps too as a result of deterioration in climatic conditions.

The standard cooking pot of earthenware or (more rarely) of metal provided the means of preparing pottage; slow cooking over several hours broke down the more intractable cereal ingredients and rendered edible the peas and beans which were often added in dried form during the lean winter months. Braising and stewing seem to have been less popular in the early medieval period; spit roasting was favoured for cooking meat, especially for feast days.

Preservation of meat through the long winter months was a major preoccupation for the cook. Venison was pressed and sealed in pots with honey to last through the closed season; beef and pork could be dry-salted or steeped in brine and hung in a dry smoky place. Dry foodstuffs such as flour and oatmeal were stored in large pottery vessels which had the advantage of being waterproof and (when suitably covered) vermin-proof. Autumn slaughtering of selected animals ensured that winter fodder had to be found for only the fittest.

Kitchen utensils were very basic and generally of iron or wood. Ladles and flesh-hooks were indispensable for serving from large cauldrons, while, for the

FIG. 41. CHIMNEY-POT or louvre, formerly mounted on the ridge of a roof in the High Street, Oxford. Smoke from the open hearth below would have escaped in a dramatic manner through its various orifices. It dates from the fourteenth century.

more ambitious cook, mortars usually of stone, were important utensils for crushing herbs and spices and in tenderising tough meat.

Dining in a medieval manor could be an elaborate and highly formal experience. Meals were served in the great hall, the lord and his guests seated at the high table on a dais at one end while the rest of the household sat on benches at trestle tables according to rank. Usually the tables were cleared away at the end of the meal, although some were more permanent. From the twelfth century the tables of the wealthy were graced with a linen cloth reaching to the floor and, instead of a plate, each person was provided with a board and a slice of 'trencher bread' to soak up the gravy from his food; this bread was not eaten by the well-off but was distributed later amongst the needy who depended on the manor for subsistence. Since guests were commonly called upon to help themselves with their fingers from a common bowl, rules concerning good behaviour and proper table manners were well developed. Cleanliness of the hands was particularly stressed, and the need for washing before and at intervals during the meal was acknowledged. Spoons had been in use since Roman times but knives designed specifically for use at table became more common only from 1500; before this time guests supplied their own knives, while table-forks were unknown until the seventeenth century.

FIG. 42. AQUAMANILE for washing the hands at table. Washing was a frequent necessity before the development of a full complement of cutlery. The vessel shown here, when complete, was in the form of a horse; lions were also popular. The water was poured through the mouth.

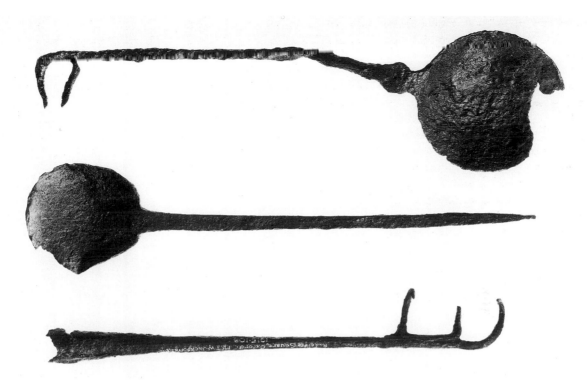

FIG. 43. KITCHEN UTENSILS of the medieval period are easily recognizable to the present-day cook. The flesh-hook for retrieving meat from a seething cauldron is now extinct, but spoons and ladles have changed little and were a necessity then as now.

FIG. 44. SAUCE BOTTLES reflect the fact that almost every medieval dish had a sauce that was considered particularly appropriate to it. These sauces were generally uncooked and were served separately from the main course on small saucers. The Ashmolean is well provided with examples.

LITERACY AND LEARNING

The impoverished state of literacy and education in King Alfred's day is revealed by the King's claim that learning had so thoroughly declined that not a single scholar south of the Thames could read or translate a letter of Latin. He wrote 'Remember what temporal punishments came upon us when we neither loved wisdom ourselves nor allowed it to others'. Alfred initiated a programme for the revival of learning both to improve religious knowledge and to promote a higher standard of pastoral care among the clergy. He attracted Latin scholars from the Continent and undertook a programme of translation so that texts would be available in English. One such text, Alfred's translation of Pope Gregory's *Pastoral Care*, survives in manuscript form in Oxford.

References to schools can be found as early as the seventh century but there was little demand except from those intended for the priesthood. The Norman Conquest brought England within the mainstream of a new era of education that spread throughout Europe in the eleventh and twelfth centuries. For example the monastic community at Canterbury was responsible for the song and grammar school to which local citizens sent their children. Throughout the Middle Ages it was the bishop of the diocese who licensed schools and teachers and delegated to a member of his clergy the appointing of the masters. However William

FIG. 45. THE MINSTER LOVELL JEWEL, although modest by comparison with its more famous contemporary the Alfred Jewel, seems to have served the same purpose: each terminates in a socket, thought to have held a pointer to aid a reader following a religious text.

FIG. 46. SEAL MATRIX of walrus ivory, incised with the figure of Saggitarius and with the name of Robert de Fontaneto. Found in Witney, it dates to the twelfth century. The use of a symbol, often a heraldic or astrological device, was of value during this period of widespread illiteracy.

FIG. 47. STYLI and other writing implements provide
tangible tokens of the spread of literacy. The stylus was used
in conjunction with a waxed tablet: the point of the stylus
inscribed the surface of the wax while the flattened end was
used to erase errors.

Boys who wished to continue their education
beyond an elementary level left home at fourteen or
fifteen to learn from a teacher reputable enough to
have established a following of students. With the protection of the Church, such scholars formed the nuclei
of what were to emerge as the universities. By 1150
there was established a body of such teachers in
Oxford. The important role of the Church in higher
education is evident in the early history of Oxford for,
as the formalised institution took shape from the loose
grouping of schools, its students, all men, had
the status of clerks in holy orders and its degrees represented a licence to teach. However, only a small
minority of ecclesiastics, whether monastic or secular,
could afford to go to the universities. In any case the
curriculum was more suited to the training of theo-
logians, canon lawyers, administrators and grammar
teachers than to that of parish priests or monks.

The support of the Pope helped to make the growing University a powerful authority within the town,
to the alarm of its inhabitants whose resentment
erupted into periodic conflict with the University
members during the thirteenth and fourteenth centuries. From each dispute, however, the University
emerged stronger as royal charters increased its privileges; the chancellor was granted almost supreme
authority over trade and a role in the policing of the
streets. In the later thirteenth century colleges for
graduate scholars were founded. Teaching was almost
entirely oral; books were scarce and expensive and
medieval libraries restricted their use by chaining the
books to the library desks.

of Wykeham in founding Winchester College in the
fourteenth century broke with tradition as this school
was to be completely independent of the Church and
the pupils were to be drawn from the poor as well as
from the nobility. The education provided by the song
school attached to a cathedral consisted, in addition to
singing, of reading, and simple instruction in the faith.
Such elementary schools provided the only academic
learning some youngsters could hope to get. For some
more fortunate boys it was also a basis for entry to the
grammar school where they would be taught mainly
Latin grammar and composition. Girls might be given
a rudimentary education but were not admitted to
grammar schools. Latin was the language of teacher
and scholar alike and was necessary for a young man
wishing to rise in society. Legal documents, wills,
deeds, and accounts and the like had to be written in
Latin and by the late twelfth century many more young
men could be employed as clerks. For many others
there would be no schooling at all and in some villages
the priest might be the only literate person in the community.

FIG. 48. SEAL MATRIX of gilt bronze (with cast) of the
University of Oxford, dating to the thirteenth century. It
was used to authenticate documents issued by the
chancellor and masters of the University. The inscription
reads SIGILL[UM] CANCELLARII ET UNIVERSITATIS
OXONIENS[IS].

RELIGION

By the time of the Viking invasions in the ninth century, England had long been wholly converted to Christianity. The building of minster churches (churches which served a monastic establishment) probably begun in the seventh or eighth century, had by then spread across the whole country bringing a measure of pastoral care to rural communities. Monasteries too were found in all areas but, because of the isolated positions which they favoured, these settlements were particularly vulnerable to attack. There is no reason to believe that the pagan Vikings looted churches and monasteries because of any specifically anti-Christian feeling; more probably they viewed them merely as rich sources for plunder. Some Scandinavian settlers were converted soon after their arrival in Britain, but in their sagas and pictorial art they continued to use the imagery of pagan myth; hence pagan figures sometimes appear on Christian monuments.

Nevertheless, the effects of the invasions and the later settlement of the Danelaw were catastrophic for the Christian church and resulted in the disappearance of most bishoprics and monasteries and almost all libraries, leading to a decline in Latin literacy. Just as Christianity on the Celtic western fringes of Britain survived both the departure of the Romans and the first Germanic invasions, so too the Church in Alfred's time survived the coming of the pagan Scandinavians, but at a cost.

How strong that Church was is open to question. In Alfred's opinion the Viking raids were a punishment from God for a people who had neglected their religious duties. He believed that his programme of educational reform was indeed necessary if there was to be an effective restoration of Christian values. The churches of the late Anglo-Saxon period could be classified under three headings: the ancient minster, the ordinary church with a graveyard, and the field-church. The field-church had no graveyard but was put up to serve new settlements which were too far

FIG. 49. TOMB SLAB fragment of the late tenth or early eleventh century, with back-biting birds inhabiting a vine scroll, found on the site of the University's Examination Schools.

FIG. 50. THE ODDA STONE, a dedication slab with a Latin text which may be translated as follows: 'Earl Odda ordered this royal church to be built and dedicated in honour of the Holy Trinity for the soul of his brother Aelfric which was taken up from this place. And Ealdred was the bishop who dedicated the same on the second of the Ides of April and in the fourteenth year of the reign of Edward, King of the English.' The stone dated by its inscription to 12th April 1056 was unearthed at Deerhurst, Gloucestershire.

FIG. 51. THE SANDFORD RELIQUARY, cast in high relief and originally gilded, depicting Christ in Majesty seated on a rainbow. The suspension loop is formed by the body of an animal. Around the side of the frame is a Latin verse reading 'May what is hidden within release us from sin'. Portable reliquaries were common, although this is the sole example in metal of the Anglo-Saxon period to survive.

FIG. 52. SEAL MATRICES of the Oxford Whitefriars (Carmelites), dating from the fourteenth century, and of the Whitefriars of Marlborough, Wiltshire. These were used to authenticate documents with the device of the prior, stamped on a wax sealing.

from the parish church to attend its services. It was, in fact, a chapel rather than a church and the parish church retained the burial fees of its parishioners.

With the tenth century there began a total reformation of the English Church. St. Dunstan (909-88), an abbot of Glastonbury who became Archbishop of Canterbury in 960, pressed for the revitalization of the monastic orders to benefit both the monasteries themselves and the pastoral mission of the Church. St. Dunstan's reformation was enacted upon the Benedictine Rule, which was followed by all English religious houses at that time. Under the Normans existing monasteries suffered comparatively little upheaval and new foundations were made by other orders – Cluniac, Cistercian and, from the twelfth century, Carthusian. In addition, houses were founded by 'canons regular' – Augustinians (black canons) and Premonstratensians (white canons) – and by the military orders of Templars and Hospitallers. Between them the monastic orders made a huge impact on society, their influence penetrating into secular as well

spiritual aspects of everyday life by virtue of the vast estates which they came to control, their patronage of the arts and crafts and their care for the physical well-being of the needy. Their increasing involvement in worldly matters tended to lead the monks away from their original spiritual mission, generating a need for periodic reforms. The most radical of these produced new communities of mendicant friars in the early thirteenth century – Dominicans, Franciscans, Carmelites and others. The friars spurned the cloistered life for one of preaching and ministering to the community at large. In the course of the fourteenth century all these orders declined: few new foundations were made after 1300 and the daughter-houses established by foreign monasteries were all dissolved during the wars with France. By 1400 the energy of the movement was spent.

In late Saxon England boundaries between the jurisdiction of Church and state were frequently blurred: bishops, for example, were appointed by the king and dispensed justice along with the earls on matters both spiritual and lay. From the tenth century the payment of tithe (one tenth of all produce of lands) by the laity was enforced by law, but it was only slowly that tithe became part of the endowment of the parish priest.

With the accession of William I the English Church was brought more into line with continental practice, although William fiercely opposed papal interference. Under Henry II the clash of interests over legal responsibility for the priesthood came to a head and brought Henry into conflict with his archbishop, Thomas Becket, whose assassination ultimately strengthened the Pope's influence as well as giving England her most famous martyr. Papal power was further enhanced when, after vain attempts at resistance, King John was forced to surrender the crown to Innocent III, receiving it back as the Pope's vassal. The influence of the papal legates, which

expanded markedly in the thirteenth century proved increasingly irksome; the secular nobility resented the power wielded by the legates at court while in the country at large there was growing dismay at the number of English benefices granted to papal favourites. The worst of these excesses were curbed in 1251 following an open revolt led by Simon de Montfort.

The Church was without doubt the great patron of the arts in medieval Europe. Whether it was for abbey, cathedral or parish church, the architecture, decoration and furnishings provided opportunities for craftsmen to glorify God with their often spectacular achievements. Gilded and painted carvings, stained-glass windows and wall paintings as well as precious ornaments and glorious vestments worn by the clergy made the Church seem a heavenly place. During the early Middle Ages it was the monks themselves who produced much of this fine craftsmanship but a

FIG. 53. PAPAL BULLAE, or leaden seals, provided a means for the medieval papacy to authenticate the documents by means of which it maintained contact with the outposts of Catholicism. In time these seals gave their name to the documents themselves, which became known as papal bulls. The bullae are standardized in appearance, bearing on one side the heads of Saints Peter and Paul and on the other the name and number of the reigning pope: those shown here are of John XXI (1276-7), Clement VI (1342-52), Innocent VI (1352-62) and Gregory XI (1370-8).

FIG. 54. LIMOGES CRUCIFIX, found in Oxford in 1704. It was recorded by Thomas Hearne, who describes the discovery of the piece, 'enamell'd and gilt with Stones in ye Arms and Brest', in gardens on the site of the church of St. Frideswide, burned by the Danes in 1002.

FIG. 55. ALABASTER PANELS mounted either singly for solitary devotion or in sets as altar-pieces formed a major vehicle for English religious art in the late Middle Ages. The above represents The Annunciation, a panel from an altar-piece depicting The Joys of the Virgin, one of the most popular themes along with The Passion of Christ.

distinction grew up between those dedicated to the religious life and lay-brothers who undertook all forms of manual labour and craftsmanship. The architectural style of eleventh-century Norman England, termed Romanesque, is distinguished by its robust and monumental columns and great rounded arches. Smaller objects too are identified with the new style; the Sandford Reliquary, for example, represents, perhaps, an important example of the early development of the Romanesque style, the earliest Norman intervention in English art, associated with the court of Edward the Confessor and pre-Conquest buildings in London and south-east England. The Gothic style introduced a new spatial experience in Church architecture; its development in France was greatly furthered in the twelfth century by Abbot Suger in the rebuilding of the east end of his church of St. Denis, north of Paris. From that time churches soared higher and higher, the pointed arch replaced the rounded Romanesque variety and the resultant lighter structure enabled walls to be opened up to include larger stained-glass windows, allowing light to stream in. All types of objects were affected by the new fashion; the niches which enclosed sculptures, the liturgical vessels, the small ivory diptychs and all types of reliquaries were among the many objects which adopted the pointed-arch style. As time went on it became even more elaborate, the arch being sometimes heavily decorated with ball-flowers and crockets. Even the humble tile-maker was influenced as can be seen on a tile from Malvern Abbey (fig 56): this particular tile was not a floor-tile but decorated the back wall of the chancel. The finest of devotional objects were made for cathedrals but by the mid-fourteenth century more emphasis was placed on the building of smaller parish churches. The more affluent layman could prepare a place for himself in heaven by financing such a foundation and the great majority of English parish churches were funded in this manner. For the patron it was necessary to make them as beautiful as possible and if he or she could not afford a fine gold cross studded with jewels, a French ivory statue or a colourful Limoges enamel casket, then he might employ local craftsmen to execute his wishes. From the second half of the fourteenth century an alternative to expensive imported white marble was found in alabaster quarried in Nottinghamshire, Derbyshire and Staffordshire. Being soft and easy to carve, it became a major medium in English religious sculpture, and was used for devotional images, tombs and altarpieces. The technical skills of the alabaster-men were not sophisticated but the effect achieved by painting and gilding made

FIG. 56. MALVERN TILE. In the middle of the fifteenth century tilers working at the Priory in Great Malvern made tiles of a very high quality for use on both walls and floors. This scene of the Resurrection would have been placed on the wall possibly, behind the high altar.

FIG. 57. AMPULLA MOULD of fine-grained limestone, found at Pirton, Worcestershire. In addition to the figures of Christ, the Virgin and St. John, a mitred figure is shown before an ecclesiastical building at the head of the cross, thought to allude to St. Thomas Becket.

44

FIG. 58. AMPULLAE (leaden bottles in which holy water could be carried home) and pilgrim badges formed the most characteristic products of the souvenir trade that developed at pilgrimage sites. Thomas Becket (martyred at Canterbury in 1170) was one of the most popular English martyrs: the badges in the upper row, the ampullae at the bottom and the 'Canterbury bells' to either side are all associated with him. Less well known was John Schorn of North Marston (Buckinghamshire) four of whose badges shown above depict the Saint with the devil captured in a boot. The scallop shell came to symbolize pilgrimage in general, although it was particularly associated with the shrine of St James at Compostella.

FIG. 59. THE BODLEIAN BOWL, of thirteenth-century date, was found in Norfolk in the seventeenth century. This bronze vessel bears a Hebrew inscription, which, though difficult to interpret, contains the information that it was the 'gift of Joseph, son the holy Rabbi Yehiel.' The bowl is apparently of French workmanship, and assuredly refers to Rabbi Yehiel of Paris, a famous Talmudic scholar, who, with his son Joseph, went to Palestine in 1260. It has in the past been assumed that the bowl may have come into England as part of some Crusader's booty but a Colchester document of 1258 records a transaction in which three of Rabbi Yehiel's sons make over to their brother Rabbi Samuel their shares in a house in Stockwell Street, left to them by their grandfather. It may well be, therefore, that the Bodleian Bowl represents a gift by Joseph to the Colchester Jews, amongst whom lived his brother.

FIG. 60. CHALICE AND PATTEN of lead, which characteristically accompanied the burials of priests from the eleventh century onwards. These symbols of priestly office were made in lead or pewter especially for interment; their discovery in medieval graves is commonplace.

FIG. 61. SHROUDED CORPSE and mortuary cross. It was common for corpses to be buried with no more than shroud or winding sheet, sometimes with a simple lead cross.

their works acceptable additions to the church, especially as devotional aids. Images of the Holy Trinity, John the Baptist or the martyrdom of particular saints were favoured but narrative scenes for the altar were also common. These altarpieces or retables consisting of sets of alabaster panels set into a wooden frame were popular, the subject matter of the narrative being frequently taken from the Easter and Christmas festivals. In England many of these altarpieces were later destroyed or at least broken up and they have survived only as single panels. Complete effigies were also made many being exported to the Continent, where they survived in better order than in post-Reformation England.

A patron regarded his church as personal property and generally reserved the right to appoint a parson. Sometimes a parish church was owned by more than one benefactor but even so in most medieval towns there were far more churches than were necessary for worship. Not surprisingly, if a church could acquire the relic of a saint it would attract pilgrims and more donations. A pilgrimage to a holy shrine, the site of martyrdom or miraculous event, formed a means of affirming faith or seeking divine intervention. Not many people could afford to journey to the holiest places like Jerusalem or Rome, nor could they undertake to go on a Crusade, but large numbers of them travelled from shrine to shrine within their own country hoping for relief from disablement and disease or for the forgiveness of sins. In medieval England the principal centres

of pilgrimage were Canterbury, scene of the murder of Thomas Becket (1170) and Walsingham where a statue of the Virgin and Child was credited with miraculous powers.

For the ordinary lay-people whose lives were full of hardship and often all too brief, the Church offered not only a space where they could practise their faith but was perhaps the one place where some beauty and colour lightened the drudgery of their existence; stained glass windows, wall paintings, the liturgy (sometimes dramatized) and mystery plays enhanced their everyday lives. It was in that very building that baptisms and funerals, the most important ceremonies of their lives were played out and it also offered a place of sanctuary in time of trouble. The Church calendar marked out the seasons for them through its festivals, holidays and fast days. Also for those who did penance and truly repented of their sins, the Church promised Christ's pardon and the certainty of an after-life where they would experience a joy perhaps unknown to them in life.

Not everyone was a Christian, however. Many Jews settled in England and played an essential role as merchants or as money-lenders (the forerunners of bankers), Christians themselves being forbidden by the Church to engage in usury. After 1290, when they were expelled by Edward I, some Jews converted to Christianity in order to stay. Heretics suffered cruel penalties, resulting in torture and frequently in death.

MEDICINE

Illness and injury could be calamities of dire seriousness in the centuries leading up to the modern period: not only were pestilence and violence more widespread but treatment was at best primitive and at times positively harmful. Already in the Anglo-Saxon period there were recognized medical men and a body of time-honoured remedies for a variety of ailments. Cures were derived from plant extracts (which might be beneficial) or from animal secretions (which were largely ineffectual). Since sickness was generally ascribed to malevolent spirits, medicines were often made deliberately obnoxious to drive the demon from the body. Importance was attached to the use of charms and amulets for the same purpose. The wealthy might protect themselves by wearing certain gems – sapphires drove away boils and swellings, jasper cured snakebites – while the less well-off made do with charm brooches.

The folk remedies of the Anglo-Saxons were to some extent displaced during the twelfth century by a resurgence of long-neglected Greek medicine, transmitted by way of influential Arab texts which began to

be translated into Latin at that time. Those medicines which provided the most effective cures derived mainly from plants, the most useful species of which were grown in monastery herb gardens, and the range of sources available was extended with overseas trade. As an alternative to herbal remedies, naturally-occurring minerals were used in the treatment of internal disorders. Clay from certain sources was used and powdered alabaster seems to have been used to treat eye problems. In medieval England two diseases were feared above all others: plague and leprosy. Plague was a general term applied to recurring epidemics that swept the country, the most virulent being the 'Black Death' of the mid fourteenth century. Leprosy was also an unspecific term encompassing a range of disorders of which true leprosy was only one. Although lepers led an unenviable existence, they enjoyed certain privileges including (for some) hospital care. Leper hospitals were unique in the service they offered to the afflicted. Hospitals were confined to monastic and charitable institutions and cared primarily for the

FIG. 62. ALABASTER of St. John the Baptist. The back is considerably worn away and an eighteenth-century inscription records that powder scraped from it was used to treat eye problems: whether the cure was attributed to the action of the mineral or to divine intervention is unrecorded.

FIG. 63. LEPER'S HEAD CORBEL, showing the horrific effects of leprosy in destroying the features. By the twelfth century there were several thousand 'lazar houses' where victims were cared for (or at least isolated) but by 1500 they had disappeared from England along with leprosy itself.

elderly and infirm. Another unpleasant disease of the times was scrofula (a tubercular infection of the lymph-nodes), commonly known as the King's Evil; many strange and horrible remedies were tried to cure sufferers. There was a superstition that to be touched by the Sovereign would bring a cure: Henry I (1100–35) claimed that he had inherited this power from his ancestor Edward the Confessor and the practice was to survive until the end of the Stuart dynasty. The custom developed that when the King performed a touching ceremony alms would also be given to the afflicted, the sum becoming fixed in the fifteenth century at one third of a pound (6s. 8d.) in the form of a new gold coin, an angel. Angels are commonly found with a hole pierced in them, since sufferers wore them around their necks as amulets. Ironically, 6s. 8d. was the recognized fee for a doctor at this time.

For common folk treatment was largely at the hands of the barbers and surgeons who formed a joint guild in London in 1493 – the first body in England to offer courses in practical anatomy. Surgical operations were of a rudimentary kind and were inevitably painful due to the lack of effective pain-killers. Apothecaries too prepared and administered medicines.

Although doctorates in medicine were awarded by the University of Oxford from the fourteenth century, the curriculum was largely theoretical and most practical physicians continued to be trained in continental schools such as Montpellier and Padua. Astrological considerations as well as conventional medical practice might be brought into play, the patient's horoscope being cast before treatment was decided upon. All these treatments had to be paid for, and so for the really impoverished the 'wise woman' of the village might be the only source of help. The most important medical school in Europe up to the twelfth century was that of the monastery of Salerno and the invention of distilling is traditionally attributed to the monks there; the process was originally developed to produce medicines rather than alcohol.

FIG. 64. CHARM BROOCHES. Those inscribed 'Ave Maria Gratia Plena' gave universal protection, while 'Jesus Nazarenus Rex' was worn against sudden death and 'Caspar, Balthazar and Melchior' provided a defence against epilepsy.

DRESS

Throughout the medieval period the lack of adequate heating in homes led both men and women to wear warm and ample layers of clothing. Dress and its ornament gave most people a means of self-expression and from the tenth century to the fifteenth there were many opportunities to introduce variety and interest into a few basic designs. Evidence for dress worn in England during the Middle Ages comes to us mainly from manuscript illuminations, effigies in stone or wood, monumental brasses, archaeological sources and wills.

The most common dress for women during the Late Saxon period included a wide-sleeved gown or robe gathered at the waist by a soft belt, an undergarment with long tight sleeves showing at the wrist and a voluminous head-dress concealing the hair and neck. Most clothes were woollen but, for the wealthy, linen undergarments and perhaps even silk gowns were a possibility. Cuffs and hems decorated with embroidery added richness and golden bands or fillets, sometimes worn around the arm or forehead were seen as status symbols. Men's costume consisted of a short woollen tunic, loose trousers and a cloak fastened by a round brooch, although more layers could be added such as a hooded coat or fur cloak.

During the years leading up to and beyond the Norman Conquest, a range of women's garments had evolved which varied in degree of elaboration rather than form. Early medieval women wore three principal garments; a close-fitting tunic or kirtle, reaching to the ground; a chemise worn below the kirtle; and an over-tunic. All of these garments were put on over the head, minimising the need for fastenings. The style was plain; the girdle at the waist being, perhaps, the richest part of the attire. The hair was always covered, except for a period in the twelfth century when long plaits, frequently extended with false hair encased in a silk bag, became fashionable. In time the outer tunic lost its sleeves and became open at the front, changing its name to a surcoat, a garment worn by both sexes. The armholes of the surcoat developed from mere slits to became larger and curved away to below the waist revealing the girdle and robe beneath. From the fourteenth century the kirtle developed a lower neck, was laced at the back and fitted to

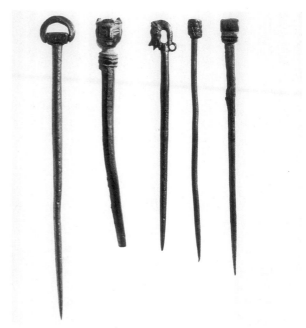

FIG. 65. PINS combined opportunities for ornament with the more practical needs of dress fastenings. Being suited to the loosely-draped clothing of the Anglo-Saxon period, they gradually lost favour with the adoption of more tightly-fitted garments in the Middle Ages, although at this period pins continued to be worn in the hair.

FIG. 66. HOOKED FASTENERS were used as general-purpose fasteners for clothing, garters, bags and the like, throughout the Late Saxon and medieval periods. The basic form is either triangular or circular; better-quality examples were made in silver with nielloed decoration.

the hip; the sleeves were belled from the elbow so that they hung to the ground, while the skirt became correspondingly fuller and trailed behind. The cote-hardie (also worn by men) gradually took over from the kirtle: it buttoned to the waist in earlier styles and by the late fourteenth century it fastened to the hem. By 1400 the principal over-garment for both men and women of fashion was the houppelande (later known as a gown); it was a long loose-fitting robe which had a very high collar and long loose wide sleeves often lined with fur or silk. In the course of the fourteenth century bodices became separated from skirts as fashion demanded tighter fastenings. Stiffened with a busk to enhance the waistline, bodices were often startlingly low-cut: a low decolletage was consid-ered a mark of chastity among the unwed, while high closed bodices were adopted by married ladies. The latter were also expected to cover their hair and they usually wore a plain white wimple with a face-framing cloth known as a gorget which was drawn into folds under the chin while a fillet or forehead-band kept the wimple in place. Head-dresses gave ample opportunity for invention and could be re-arranged in many extraordinary ways. Such changes in fashion were not within the reach of ordinary country-women who continued to wear loose gowns to the ankles and their hair covered in a wimple of coarse linen.

FIG. 68. BRASS-RUBBING. Margaret Peyton (1484) of Isleham, Cambridgeshire is portrayed wearing an elegant low-necked gown, apparently of rich brocade or cut velvet, with large, turned-back cuffs. Her elaborate headdress is decorated with the words 'Lady Help Ihesu Mercy'.

FIG. 67. LATE MEDIEVAL CORBEL, (rafter support), representing a figure with a cowled head-dress.

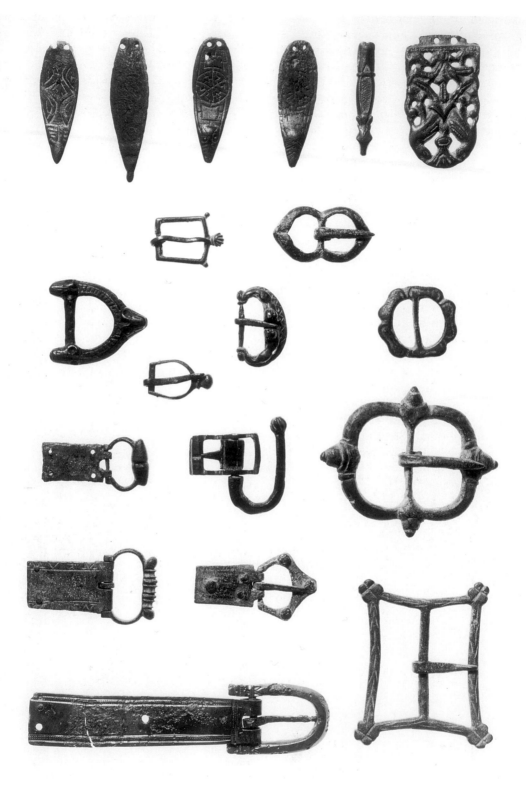

FIG. 69. STRAP-ENDS AND BUCKLES from leather belts are common finds on archaeological excavations. The free end of the belt was usually mounted with an ornamental chape or strap-end: all those shown here (top) are of late Saxon date. In both single and double buckles, the form of the loop (or frame) provides a basis for dating: those illustrated range from the twelfth to the fourteenth or fifteenth century.

52

The basic outfit for men at the time of the Norman Conquest consisted of a knee-length short-sleeved tunic, with a long-sleeved linen shirt beneath. The 'braes' (breeches) were tied with cross-bands from knee to ankle. Clothes however played an important part in asserting one's place in society and soon cloaks might have fur-lining and tunics, which swept the ground, their edges ornamented with coloured bands of embroidery. Men from the upper ranks of society dressed in long, full tunics under a sleeveless surcoat (at first in its simplest form it was worn by men over armour) and a voluminous cloak, both of which reached to the feet, although lengths could vary according to personal choice. This underlined the fact that they did not work in the fields like peasants, but for more active pursuits like hunting they might wear a tunic ending at the knee over which was a cloak of about the same length. The fourteenth century saw the beginning of more shapely and better-cut clothes. The use of fastenings such as buttons, laces or hooks-and-eyes allowed tight-fitting clothes to be worn. Breeches fell out of fashion and men began to wear hose of bright colours. Around 1335 the tunic was replaced by a doublet, or gipon, worn over a shirt and shaped to fit the waist. Jackets and jerkins replaced the cote-hardie around 1450. The hood was the principal head-covering for men and at one period it developed a peak so long that it reached to the ground. This fashion led to much experimentation resulting in some extraordinary headgear.

The peasantry dressed in a manner most fitted to their surroundings and occupations. Little changed from late Saxon times to the fourteenth century and forms were basic. Within a village most probably all clothing needs would be met by the local women who would spin and weave wool and flax. Sheepskin would serve to give added warmth in winter and the hides of sheep provided soft leather for more waterproof hoods. Men protected their legs with twisted straw wrapped round their breeches if they did not have leather to make cross-garters. It was more in the quality of the material and in degree of elaboration

FIG. 70. SHOES AND PATTENS. Shoes were made throughout the medieval period by the turnshoe method, constructed inside-out on a last, stitched along the seams and made without separate heels. Their ability to withstand the wet was limited: Wooden pattens or overshoes, sometimes raised on iron supports, provided a measure of protection.

that their clothes differed from those of their superiors. As towns and manufacturing capacity grew in the later fourteenth century clothes and materials became cheaper and it became easier for the peasant to acquire an outfit with some cut and style.

Wool textiles were the most commonly used fabric but linen was also available. Flax was grown in England but the best quality linen was imported from abroad. Everyone who could afford it wore linen for underwear and women used it for wimples and aprons. To have a large supply of clean white linen was a reflection of wealth and status as it required frequent laundering. It is interesting to note that whilst outer clothing was unlikely to be cleaned, linen was washed regularly. The services of a laundress would be required to deal with the enormous quantity of linen used by a large household, which of course also included table and bed linen.

Leather provided the best material for boots, shoes, gloves, and belts and was mostly obtained from the skins of domesticated animals. Gloves were worn by all sections of society and the giving of gloves as gifts was a general custom. All footwear was made by the turnshoe method of construction, in which shoes were sewn inside-out and reversed for wear. There grew a custom for pointed toes which could be stuffed with material; the style went to absurd lengths in the late fourteenth century when the points were so long that they were tied back to the knees. Shoes too could be made of finer materials and sewn with pearls or the leather might be stamped with gold. To protect

FIG. 71. LINEN SMOOTHER or 'slick-stone' of glass used to smooth textiles. The earliest examples come from the Viking period and they remained in use in England until the late medieval period. This example probably belongs with these later types.

such footwear when worn out-of-doors pattens were developed, consisting of a wooden sole with a leather band which fitted over the shoe; the wearer was raised off the ground by several inches on an iron frame.

Returning Crusaders introduced richer materials into England – cotton, muslin (from Mosul), damask (from Damascus) and gauze (from Gaza) – all of which transformed medieval costume for the rich who now dressed in a more exotic way. For instance women's veils became gauzy and hung from steeple-shaped or horned head-dresses.

Rich embroidery of silk or gold thread-work formed an important part of the decoration of regal and ecclesiastical clothing and achieved in England a standard that was unmatched elsewhere. Although the embroideries which survive are largely ecclesiastical in origin there was, no doubt, a considerable amount of secular work but it was not until the Tudor period that the middle classes could afford such luxury.

Although finger-rings have been worn in Britain since Roman times, it is only from the late Saxon period that we have evidence for the wearing of particularly fine rings by people of some status. They were nearly all of gold and, in comparison with the comparatively modest examples of twisted wire or sheet metal recovered from many Saxon graves, demonstrate how rings had become a prestigious item of decoration. In the middle of the fourteenth century they became a real status symbol with decrees that they could be worn legally only by the upper classes. Sumptuary laws governing dress codes usually proved totally ineffective, but not entirely. However there was now a necessity for a growing number of people to wear signet rings with which to authenticate documents, so merchants and lesser landowners might own rings along with those of more noble rank. Wills and inventories seem to indicate that some people might own several rings, each of which performed a different function – religous or magical, for example, or as personal tokens of affection.

The ornament most common to both sexes was the brooch, which was practical in the sense that it might hold the clothing together as well as being decorative. Everyday brooches of the Late Saxon and Viking period were commonly discoid, some taking their form from coins; annular or ring-shaped brooches dominated all others in the medieval period. The simplest sometimes had an incised motto or punched decoration, while more elaborate 'cluster brooches' were mounted with imitation gems in paste or glass. This basic form survived to

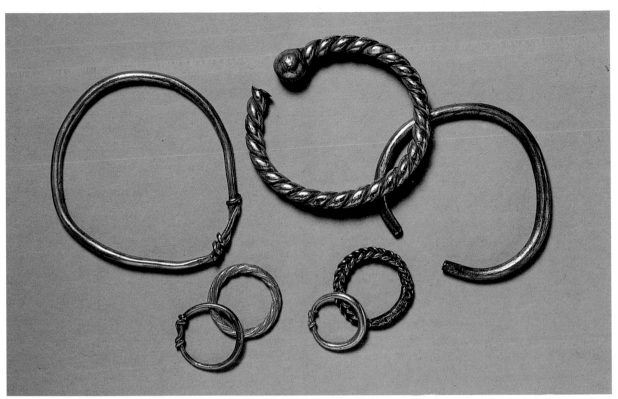

FIG. 72. SILVER & GOLD JEWELLERY. Silver was the most widely used precious metal in the Viking period. The popular twisted or plaited, slip-knot and plain designs are represented here by bracelets. Gold ornaments occur less frequently but as the twisted finger-ring demonstrates similar designs were used.

FIG. 73. RINGS from the Thame Hoard, found in 1940 by the edge of the River Thame. Two of the rings are set with stones (turquoise and toad-stone) thought to have magical properties, one is a plain hoop bearing a personal inscription, one with a faceted peridot may be ecclesiastical while a magnificent reliquary ring set with a double-armed cross of amethyst and engraved on the back with the Crucifixion is one of the most splendid medieval rings to survive. Ten silver groats found with the rings give a terminal date of 1457.

the end of the medieval period, most being made of bronze and more rarely of silver. Popular late medieval variants featuring a pair of clasped hands are interpreted as love tokens, while others display a variety of pleasingly decorative forms.

As well as the growth or ornamentation in dress and jewellery, objects of everyday use became more decorative throughout the Middle Ages. The earliest combs, for example, are generally of composite construction, and made of antler; most carry schematic decoration or occasionally interlace or animal ornament in the Anglo-Saxon and Viking period. These were displaced by more practical single-piece products in the early medieval period, most commonly in cattle horn, bone or box-wood. Later combs developed into objects of beauty, executed in ivory and sometimes showing courtly scenes. No less beautiful were the mirror-cases also carved in ivory and showing similar scenes. These carved images of medieval life provide an illustration of how colourful and elaborate dress and ornament had become by the fifteenth century.

FIG. 74. IVORY MIRROR-CASE carved with lovers meeting in a garden between two trees, squared at the corners with four crouching monsters. French or English, early fourteenth century.

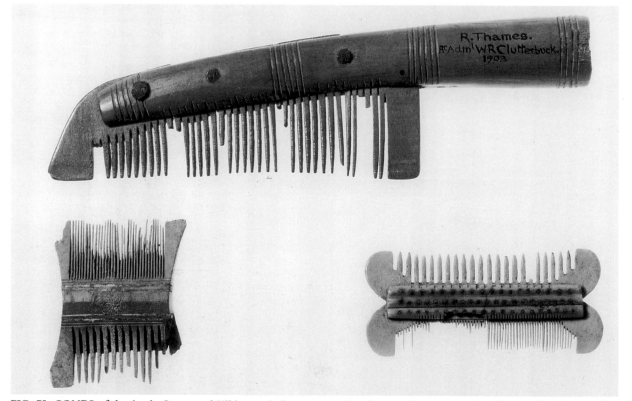

FIG. 75. COMBS of the Anglo-Saxon and Viking period were normally of composite construction. The handled form, with several tooth-plates riveted into a slotted antler tine, provides an alternative to those composed with riveted side-plates; multiple rivets of bronze characterize the latest combs in this series. One-piece combs become universal from the end of the twelfth century, sometimes of bone but increasingly of horn and box-wood. Ivory remained a luxury material throughout the Middle Ages.

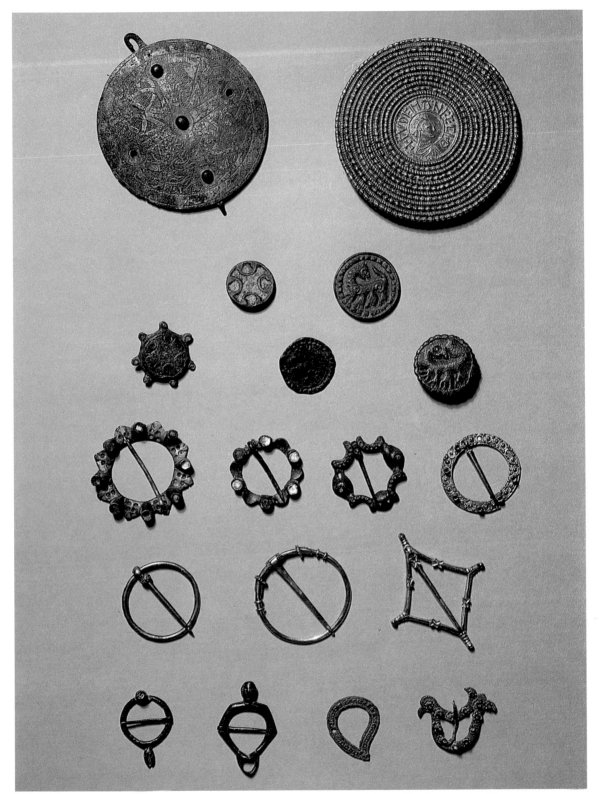

FIG. 76. BROOCHES formed as discs account for a large proportion of the medieval repertoire. The ornament may be incised, cast or enamelled; coins continue to form a basis for some - a long-standing tradition. Annular (or ring-shaped) brooches also enjoyed wide popularity, often embellished with fake gemstones of paste.

SPORTS AND PASTIMES

Games have always provided a form of release from the more burdensome aspects of everyday life and in the medieval period sports tended to be violent in nature and played with passion. Ball games have had a long popularity and formerly were played by large numbers of participants at a time; contests might involve teams consisting of entire villages pitched against each other and were conducted on a basis akin to tribal warfare, occasionally involving life-threatening skirmishes. Both feet and hands were used in these ball games but as various pieces of equipment were added new sports evolved, among which were the predecessors of modern golf, hockey, cricket and bowls. Legislation also helped to shape the form of such games, since measures were introduced from time to time to limit excessive violence; these moves were motivated partly by concern at the attendant dangers but more importantly by alarm at the distractions they caused from all-important archery practice.

A greater degree of refinement was brought to ball games when enclosed areas or courts became fashionable venues for games; more sophisticated equipment such as rackets were introduced and more formalized rules were devised. While the game of tennis became a popular aristocratic sport at the end of the medieval period, handball, the popular equivalent, was still played in the open spaces by all other classes.

Wrestling enjoyed a popularity grounded in the attractions of gambling, when locals backed their man against the visiting opponent. The wrestling matches took place in any available public arena, including churchyards; they were very violent and occasionally deaths are recorded. It was common for a fight to have a group of contestants in the ring which made for an exciting spectacle for the spectators who were always vociferous and frequently riotous.

Archery as a sport was everywhere encouraged since it helped provide trained bowmen in time of military need. The sport was so popular that it was practised by both sexes and by all classes. To encourage archers royal statutes subsidized the sale and manufacture of longbows and a bowman who killed someone accidently while practising at the butts was declared immune of the charge of murder. The crossbow never

FIG. 77. BALL GAMES could be violent in character, as in this illustration from Bede's Life of St Cuthbert of c.1120-30. The boy St Cuthbert, too fond of playing games, is warned in a vision to be more serious. (Bodleian Library, Oxford MS University College. 165, p.8.)

FIG. 78. HAWKING enjoyed huge popularity in aristocratic circles up to the seventeenth century. This thirteenth-century knife-handle in the form of a young noble with a hawk at the wrist, represents an embodiment of refinement, for through the limitation of hawking to the nobility the hawk itself became a symbol of rank.

achieved the status of the longbow in English archery but was popular with women and boys, who found it a suitable weapon to use when fowling.

The tournament or tourney was already popular in France in Norman times but in England the first evidence dates from Henry III's reign. The first tournaments were no more than bloody mêlées where knights and would-be-knights hoping to improve their skill in armed combat could practise military manoeuvres and show their prowess. The violence which characterized the earlier medieval period gave way in time to chivalric jousts between just two contestants. By the reign of Edward III both tournaments and jousts were conducted according to a strict code of chivalry and gave opportunity for extravagant displays of spectacular costume and armour. No less splendid would be the horses and the heralds who announced and supervised the tournaments.

Not everyone could own a horse but horse racing became popular from the sixteenth century at the latest and appealed to all classes: up to the later seventeenth

FIG. 79. BIRD LURE of green-glazed pottery. After camouflaging himself, the hunter would blow on this whistle to stimulate the curiosity of his prey and to attract it within easy range.

FIG. 80. KNIGHTLY COMBAT is wonderfully captured on this double-sided chess-piece of walrus ivory. It portrays two mounted warriors each wearing a great helm, a mail shirt under a surcoat, and mail hose; each carries a shield. Traces of gilt survive on the belts and harness of both figures and on the shield of one of them; traces of dark pigment can be seen on the mail armour of both and may also originally have covered their helms. Current opinion identifies it as English workmanship of the thirteenth century. (See also back cover)

century virtually all such competitions were two-horse races, but betting was no less intense for that.

For the privileged few, hunting for game such as deer provided the supreme sport; wild boar were hunted to extinction in Britain in the course of the medieval period. Vast tracts of deer forest were maintained for the Crown and for fortunate noblemen and ecclesiastics with hunting rights. Special regulations were enacted to protect the beasts of the forest from all but their legal pursuers; harsh punishments, often in the form of crippling fines, were meted out to those found poaching.

Hawking was enjoyed by both sexes and ownership of a hawk was a status symbol. Native peregrine falcons were highly prized at home and abroad, though the Normans brought new breeds and more sophisticated customs to the sport.

More accessible to ordinary folk, especially in towns, was bear-baiting, in which the bear was chained to a post before having fierce dogs set upon it, with inevitable injury or death on either side. Bulls were also regularly chained and baited, the contest in this instance taking place in the municipal bullring. Typically this was usually sited near the 'shambles' or

FIG. 81. MUZZLED BEAR, carved on a corbel (rafter support). Bears had to be imported from the Continent and their high value meant that many found themselves in corporate ownership.

FIG. 82. MEDIEVAL HUNTING ARROWS are traditionally said to be distinguished by their long trailing barbs although more recently the distinction between sporting and military forms has become less clear. Even the forked variety, formerly associated with hunting birds and other game, is now claimed as an anti-personnel weapon.

60

butchers' quarter. After the contest it was the fate of the bull to be consumed.

The winter months, when ponds, rivers and water-meadows froze over, brought the outdoor pleasure of skating. Skates were made from animal bones and the skater propelled himself with a spiked pole. Since the leg-bones favoured for these skates were readily available, the sport was hugely popular; metal-bladed skates were introduced only in the sixteenth century. Even skating could be seen as a preparation for war: an eleventh-century account of winter sports at Moorfields in London describes how pairs of skaters would challenge each other with their poles raised like lances, often resulting in broken limbs and other injuries.

More gentle pastimes were provided by board-games such as tables (a form of backgammon), chess and, particularly among the lower class, merels or nine-men's-morris. The latter took many forms but the simplest consisted of nine holes carved out of whatever flat surface was available – sometimes benches or pews. Players had three pieces each, which they put down alternately, trying to get three in a row, as in noughts and crosses. Chess was the most popular

board game, combining mental stimulus and a challenge which was met with the same eagerness as the physical bouts in the tournament. The game which may have been played first in India came to Britain via the Muslim world (including Spain) and France and was being eagerly contested by the mid-twelfth century.

Dicing was popular but card-playing was largely a courtly pastime until the later fifteenth century, when printed cards became available. Both of these games encouraged gambling, which has a long history as an addictive pastime.

Music-making was also widely popular. Many noble households hired their own minstrels to provide entertainment. Otherwise, two main classes of entertainers are recognized – those who recited romances and travelling players with their bawdy songs and comic acts. Having no permanent theatres, ordinary folk would enjoy wandering musicians, jugglers and acrobats at fairs or on market days. In the late fourteenth century some of the guilds began to perform mystery plays in certain towns. These were processional performances using pageant wagons paid for by the craft guilds and arising directly from the

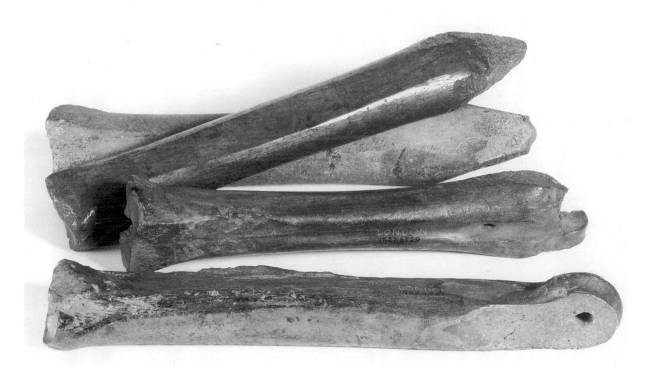

FIG. 83. BONE SKATES were easily produced from the leg bones of horses and cattle. A flat sliding surface was produced by grinding the bone on a stone. Some were pointed and upswept at the toe; they might also be perforated for bindings. The skater pushed himself along with a spiked pole, as though skiing.

Church's desire to engage the people more actively with their faith. Real understanding of the Latin services of the Church was limited largely to the clergy and perhaps a few of the laity, plays, written in the vernacular, were instructive as well as entertaining: this form of theatre was a community art where every member of society could play his part. In York, for example, the cycle of plays performed for the feast of Corpus Christi would have included a large percentage of the population, each guild being responsible for one pageant in the story. The performance began at 4.30am and lasted until 9.00pm; there is evidence that it was accompanied by a great deal of eating, drunkenness, shouting and singing, much to the chagrin of the clergy.

It would seem that, whether playing games, competing at sports, making music, play-acting or simply spectating, there was in the medieval character a vigour and exuberance which reflects an attitude to life which we may find also in the artefacts and buildings they made.

FIG. 84. WHISTLE, JEW'S HARP AND TUNING PEGS. Simple instruments as represented by these fragments formed (together with the drum) the most accessible means of music-making in the fourteenth century.

FIG. 85. GAMING PIECES. During the eleventh and twelfth centuries large numbers of playing pieces were produced for the game of 'tables', in response to a seemingly insatiable public appetite for the game. Tablemen for everyday use were made of bone or antler often decorated with no more than incised ring-and-dot or geometrical motifs while more expensive tastes were catered for by elaborately carved ivory pieces, frequently, as here (top), of walrus ivory: these show St. Martin dividing his coat with a beggar.

BIBLIOGRAPHY

J. Alexander and P. Binski (eds.), 1987. *The Age of Chilvary: Art in Plantagenet England 1200-1400*, exhibition catalogue, Royal Academy (London).

J. Backhouse, D.H. Turner and L. Webster (eds.), 1984. *The Golden Age of Anglo-Saxon Art*, exhibition catalogue, British Museum (London).

J. Blair, 1994. *Anglo-Saxon Oxfordshire* (Stroud).

J. Blair and N. Ramsay (eds.), 1991. *English Medieval Industries* (London).

D.C. Calthrop, 1946. *English Costume 1066-1820* (London).

J. Campbell (ed.), 1982. *The Anglo-Saxons* (Oxford).

F. Cheetham, 1984. *English Medieval Alabasters*, Victoria & Albert Museum (London).

J. Cherry, 1991. *Medieval Decorative Art*, British Museum (London).

H. Clarke, 1984. *The Archaeology of Medieval England* (London).

J. Cowgill *et al.*, *Knives and Scabbards* (Medieval Finds from Excavations in London 1) (London).

D.W. Crossley, 1981. *Medieval Industry* (CBA Research Report 40) (London).

H.R. Ellis Davidson, 1962. *The Sword in Anglo-Saxon England* (Oxford).

E.S. Eames, 1985. *English Tilers*, British Museum, (London).

W.L. Goodman, 1962. *The History of Woodworking Tools* (London).

A. MacGregor, 1985. *Bone, Antler, Ivory and Horn* (London).

T. MacLean, 1984. *The English at Play in the Middle Ages* (Windsor Forest).

M. Mellor, 1994. *Oxfordshire Pottery* (Oxford).

A.R. Myers, 1952. *England in the Late Middle Ages* (London).

C. Platt, 1978. *Medieval England* (London).

J.D. Richards, 1991. *Viking Age England* (London).

F.G. Skinner, 1967. *Weights and Measures: their ancient origins and their development in Great Britain up to AD 1855* (London).

J. Steane, 1985. *The Archaeology of Medieval England and Wales* (London).

D.M. Stenton, 1951. *English Society in the Early Middle Ages* (London).

D.M. Wilson, 1976. *The Archaeology of Anglo-Saxon England* (London).

ILLUSTRATIONS

Fig.1: 1836.371 (Newton Park, Som.). Fig.3: 1886.443/4 (Oxf.). Fig.4: 1978.332 (up.). Fig.5: 1685 A 600 (up.). Fig.6: 1954.673 (up.). Fig.7: 1890.14 (Abingdon). Fig.8: Swords, 1914.456 (Thames,Oxon.); 1985.48 (Crowmarsh); Loan 294 (Pitt Rivers); Knives, 1941.82 (Brackley); 1914.454 (Thames,Oxon.); Winged Spearhead 1975.345. Fig.10: 1995.402 (Wilts); 1879.255 (up.); 1896.1904 R4 (Woodeaton); 1888.1393 g, 1888.1393c, 1888.1393 (up.). Fig 11: Swords, 1955.412 (Baydon); 1885.757 (Thames); 1836.68p7; 1949.961; Daggers, 1836.68p8 (Sandford); 1880.266 (Oddington); 1950.235 (Lewes). Fig.12: 1887.3010 (Standlake); 1886.581 (Witney); 1909.414 (Mildenhall); Loan 393; 1990.92 (Bradford-on-Avon); 1995.74 (up.); 1876.95 (Islip); 1886.445 (Oxf.). Fig.13: 1961.423 (York); 1886.1232 (Oxf.); 1914.455 (Shifford); 1955.398 (Slaughterford); 1886.580 (Radcot); 1869.32 (Marlow); 1910.297, 1887.2553 (Oxf.). Fig.14: 1991.144 (Seacourt); 1971.1218 (Aldbourne); 1991.143 (Seacourt). Fig.15: 1909.519-551 (Ribble Valley). Fig.18: 1929.662 (Crete); 1950.291 (up.); 1927.6529 (Bury.St Edmunds); 1924.504 (Blewbury); 1896.1908 M100 (Ixworth). Fig.19: 1984.112 (Faversham); 1927.6360 (Stourbridge, Cambs.). Fig.21: 1888.106 (Oxf.). Fig.22: 1951.4354 (Oxf.). Fig.24: 1991.136, 1921.190 (Oxf.). Fig.25: 1972.20 (up.). Fig.26: 1969.101, 1969.102, 1977.35 (Seacourt). Fig.27: 1913.909 (Oxford); 1955.428 (Liddington Castle); 1889.190, 1889.189 (up.); 1873.55, 1873.56 (Woodperry). Fig.28: 1991.139 (Oxf.). Fig.29: 1991.135 (up.); 1913.915 (Oxf.); 1982.532; 1991.134 (up.). Fig.30: 1917.25, 1917.25a (Crowmarsh); 1890.34, 1876.30, 1876.32 (Oxf.); 1910.301 (Beckley). Fig.31: 1938.1174, 1938.1173 (Oxf.) 1878.267 (Osney); 1911.515 (Howberry); 1894.25 (up.); 1836p133 No.335 (Lichfield); 1887.2548 (Winslow); 1936.120 (Oxf.); 1873.187 (Thames Oxon.); 1959.160 (Oxf.); 1873.65, 1873.66 (Woodperry); 1969.123 (Seacourt); 1991.141, 1938.883 (Oxf.). Fig.32: 1909.518 (Windsor); 1970.1067 (Bossington); 1930.639, 1935.3, 1930.638 (up.) 1930.636 (Coggeshall). Fig.33: M187,1907, 1887.3072 (Oxf.); Loan 306 (Chaddesley Corbett); 1909.425 (West Stow); 1992.99 (Bergh Apton); 1920.60 (Wilcote); 1995.74 (up.). Fig.34: 1886.1679, 1956.278, M9, 1935.6, 1991.55, 1935.8, 1912.30 (Oxf.). Fig.35: 1923.261 (Middle Aston); 1873.7 (Woodperry.); 1927.5965c (Harlton); 1927.5965i (Scampston); 1991.137 (up.); 1883.44 (Oxf.); 1909.834 (Beauvais); 1991.138 (up); 1927.6580 (Harlton); 1880.143 (Barnwell). Fig.36: M189; 1959.197, 1909.907, 1966.226, 1984.1183, 1997.21 (Oxf.). Fig.37: M8, 1888,107, 1891.6, M62, 1921.202 (Oxf.). Fig.39: 1921.317, M133, 1935.602, 1874.29, M 120 (Oxf.). Fig.40: 1921.210, 1915.79, 1937.888, 1895.71 (Oxf.). Fig.41: 1887.3206 (Oxf.). Fig.42: 1955.480 (Oxf.). Fig.43: 1915.108 (Oxf.); 1964.184 (up.); 1971.1178 (Brandon). Fig 44: 1872.2430, 1921.203, 1921.204, 1836.68p17, M2,1908 (Oxf.). Fig.45: 1869.20 (Oxon.). Fig.46: 1939.463 (Witney). Fig.47: 1927.806 (Icklingham); 1921.1047 (Abingdon); 1927.816 (Icklingham); 1887.3327 (up.). Fig.48: Loan 114, M1172 (Oxf.). Fig.49: 1876.94 (Oxf.). Fig.50: 1909.1212, M300 (Deerhurst). Fig.51: 1891.10 (Sandford). Fig.52: R14, 1836p142 no.406a (up.). Fig.53: M99 (Ipsden); 1985.233(up.); 1938.16 (Bicester); 1955.391 (Swindon). Fig.54: 1887.2391 (Oxf.); Fig.55: Loan 99 (up.). Fig.56: 1967.672 (Malvern). Fig.57: Loan 370 (Pirton). Fig.58: 1988.397, 1989.569 (up.); 1986.2 (Billingsgate); 1927.6409 (Icklingham); 1997.13, 1997.6 (Lon.); 1921.189 (Horspath); 1997.11 (up.); 1997.14 (Lon.); 1927.6411, 1927.6412, 1987.149, 1987.150 (Thames, Lon.). Fig.59: Loan 385 (Norfolk). Fig.60: 1836p133 No.349 (Sandford). Fig.61: 1927.6476 (Horncastle); 1869.8 (Oxf.). Fig.62: 1685 A325e (up.). Fig.63: 1936.225 (up.). Fig.64: 1927.6278, 1927.6282, 1927.6288, 1836.68, 1927.6279, 1927.6283, 1927.6289, 1974.294, 1927.6285, 1987.6281, 1927.6287 (up.). Fig.65: 1927.107 (Ireland); M113 1908 (Oxf.); 1924.777 (Ireland); 1972.18 (up.); 1927.6514 (Cambridge). Fig.66: 1991.29 (Aston Bampton & Shifford); 1927.6381 (St. Albans); R156 (Woodeaton); 1887.3305 , 1987.18 (up.). Fig.67: 1985.53 (up.); Fig. 69: 1940.11 (Burford); 1975.305 (Owmby); 1927.124, 1927.125 (Sutherland); 1909.442, 1909.446 (Ixworth); 1927.6314 (Malton); 1950.287 (Colchester); 1927.6372 (Old Sarum); 1927.6220 (Kent); 1921.294 (Oxford); 1927.6304 (Dunwich); 1927.6263 (Cambs.); 1873.184 (Oxf.); 1958.258 (up.); 1927.6257 (Suffolk); 1911.517 (Crowmarsh); 1927.6231 (Suffolk); 1991.304 (Dorchester). Fig.70: Shoes 1957.68, 1957,69 (Oxf.); Pattens, 1987.16, 1987.17 (up.). Fig.71: 1993.89 (Didcot). Fig.72: 1932.892 (Ireland); 1957.61 (Long Wittenham); 1909.552 (Ireland); 1930.643 (Thetford); 1930.627 (Suffolk); 1930.629 (Ixworth); 1996.268 (up.). Fig.73: 1940.224-228 (Thame). Fig.74: 1656p38, 1685 A No.585 (up.). Fig.75: 1987.15 (Thames); 1915.88 (Oxf.); 1967.1091 (Denmark). Fig.76: 1979.79 (Leicester); 1951.131 (Canterbury); 1927.254 (Pakenham); 1909.459 (Icklingham); 1992.97 (Mildenhall); 1909.465 (Icklingham); Loan 315; 1927.6291 (Scarborough); 1927.6290 (up.); 1927.6299 (Dunwich); 1991.5 (Blackthorn); 1927.6325 (Norwich); 1994.26 (Dorchester); 1994.28 (up.); 1869.6 (Littlegate); 1927.6310, 1927.6339, 1927.6294 (Ixworth). Fig.78: 1886.13a (Oxf.). Fig.79: 1910.310 (Oxf.). Fig.80: 1685 A587 (up.). Fig.81: 1995.40 (up.). Fig.82: 1986.20 (up.); 1889.47 (Witney); 1967.906 (up.); 1936.119 (Deddington); 1879.248 (Blenheim). Fig.83: 1981.66 (Lon.). Fig.84: 1977.135 (Seacourt); 1873.97 (Woodperry); 1921.1050 (Woodeaton); Loan 407 (Oxf.). Fig.85: 1656p38 1685 A No.588-589 (up.); 1953.128 (Scandinavia); 1967.452, 1967.453 (Oxf.).

Front cover: Limoges enamel chasse, showing martyrdom and burial of St.Thomas: M255.
Back cover: ivory chessman, 1685 A 587.

ABBREVIATIONS. Cambs: Cambridgeshire;Lon: London; Oxf: Oxford; Oxon: Oxfordshire; Som: Somerset; up: unprovenanced.